KB265691

Valuation of hotel

내일을여는지식 / 경영경제 3

- Food & Beverage department -

Valuation of hotel

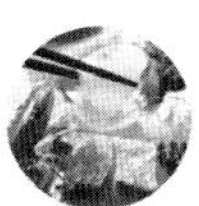  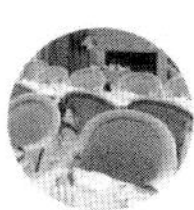

김기영 · 이재철 · 정성훈 지음

KSi 한국학술정보[주]

Nowadays, the fundamental purpose of hotel industry management is to produce significant profits. Therefore, in order to achieve the purpose, it is necessary not only to grasp a value of the company but also, to manage the hotel efficiently as analysing a value.

For the Hotel company to adapt the efficient management environment, it has to focus on internal growth rather than external growth, thus, customer satisfaction management based on long term competitive power is a short-cut of maximizing the business value.

Hotel industry is the service industry to satisfy the customer's basic needs, and has been developed according to economic development as well as increasing of income level and change of life patterns.

However, the most important aim of hotel industry is expanding industry scale and market share through growth of sales in order to increase profit Hotel industry recognized the limitation of growth focused on external size after going through IMF finance crisis and gained interest in increasing profit. CEOs of industry showed more interest in profitability and financial integrity than the external appearance.

Concrete aim for this study is as followed. Firstly, examining the theory frame of DCF analysis method among hotel related company value evaluation method of advanced countries; secondly, verifying whether the DCF model is rational and systemic value evaluating method for domestic hotel companies with suitable hotel F&B management strategy of our country; and thirdly, comparing basic business evaluating method of current hotel − related business with evaluating method through DCF model for accurate quantitative judgement regarding the adequate value evaluation method of F&B facilities.

Aim of this study is calculating the value by DCF model that has been applied for general manufacturing companies and applying it in management strategy of hotel F&B related facilities, calculating DCF value based on financial statement, income statement and cash flow statement used in hotel companies and using this value, accurately analyzing F&B facilities of hotel company to predict future profit using the most universal method for working out the profit value. The main aim is to suggest the significance and possibility of practical application of study results and direction for future studies.

This study is made through research literature, internal and external references and data, company value evaluation theories and, research papers about company value evaluation of hotels and companies related with hotels and etc. And also, as using DCF model, we collect Financial Statement of A hotel and B hotel, and Income Statement of food and beverage. In addition, as selecting 14 business places in A hotel, and 7 business places in B hotel in Seoul for empirical analysis.

Based on the main financial statement and the market data from 2001. 01. to 2007. 12, the subjected hotels are selected and analyzed.

Company value of hotels was applied adequately for domestic situation based on DCF model and it was calculated, analyzed also by using DCF model. Also, analysis subjected companies were limited to currently operating F&B facilities and value of hotel F&B facilities was evaluated for comparative analysis regarding 2 hotels that are operating F&B facilities, other facilities and banquet hall.

This study comparatively analyzed asset and future value of F&B facilities through observation status and formation of domestic hotel industry.

Chapter 1 is the introduction part to state the problems, purposes, methods and structure of this study.

Chapter 2 is the statement part to explain the concept of business value as the theoretical background of company value evaluation and company value evaluation model. And also, foreign and domestic studies are considered.

Chapter 3 addresses the data collection, the analysis method, and the study model of Korean hotel companies.

Chapter 4 analyzes business value using Discounted Cash Flow and Hamada model, the evaluation model for this study. Also, to perform comparative evaluation of model value and future value, business value was evaluated by classifying as sample hotel F&B facility. Lastly, NPV(Net present value) value and future estimated profit rate of sample hotel businesses were comparatively evaluated.

Chapter 5 is the conclusion part to summarize the result of this study. Suggestion and limitation of this study and future study plan are addressed.

The study used 2 hotel firms as an analyze sample to introduce a new reasonable valuation model that can evaluate the current value of hotel businesses and from these 2 samples, we extracted data from January, 2001 to December, 2007. These data include financial statements of each firm and the income statement and cash flow statement of each place of business. The 7 years period data was used to create a valuation model for each office. Estimated NOPAT, net working capital, NPV, estimated period and discount rate were used as variables for evaluating the value of each place of business and the discounted cash flow model was used to discount and calculate the remaining value. These 2 values were then added up to accurately draw the total value of each place of business.

The parameter data used in this method were all mainly extracted from Korea's food service industry and applied to the model, enabling realistic evaluation.

The DCF Model used in the study showed the value for each place of business of hotel A and hotel B. Hotel B received better results and was generally valuated to possess a high financial validity for most of its values. In specific, out of 14 business places of hotel A, which are 8 food service, 3 beverage service, 1 banquet hall and 2 others, 4 business places were valuated to have financial validity. For hotel B, 2 food service, 2 beverage service, 1 banquet hall and 2 others, 6 business places had financial validity and 1 had low financial validity, showing that hotel B's future value will be higher than hotel A.

First, as a method of the study, accurate data is essential for using the research model to correctly valuate the current and future value of hotel businesses and to plan a future management strategy and these data will enable to question the reasonableness of the valuation results. Therefore, the study will be able to provide information and help to those managers planning to invest in the hotel industry.

Second, future studies should be conducted on the research of creating a DCF Model that can include non−financial variables in its analyze and also the techniques required for the model.

Therefore, continuous future studies are required to apply the DCF Model method to Korea's hotel industry. Also, as the hotel industry is yet in the phase of growth, in order to increase the reasonableness and accuracy of business valuation, new models and methods based on various businesses, new projects and management strategies should be created. These studies will be able to invent a perfect model for valuating business developments and each place of business.

차 례 C o n t e n t s

Chapter 01　**Introduction**

Valuation of hotel — Food & Beverage department —

Introduction

1 Statement of Problem of the Study

1) Statement of Problem

Nowadays, the fundamental purpose of hotel industry management is to produce significant profits. Therefore, in order to achieve the purpose, it is necessary not only to grasp a value of the company but also, to manage the hotel efficiently as analysing a value.

For the Hotel company to adapt the efficient management environment, it has to focus on internal growth rather than external growth, thus, customer satisfaction management based on long term competitive power is a short-cut of maximizing the business value.

Hotel industry is the service industry to satisfy the customer's basic needs, and has been developed according to economic development as well as increasing of income level and change of life patterns.

However, the most important aim of hotel industry is expanding industry scale and market share through growth of sales in order to increase profit

Hotel industry recognized the limitation of growth focused on external size after going through IMF finance crisis and gained interest in increasing profit. Chief Executive Officers(CEOs) of industry showed more interest in profitability and financial integrity than the external appearance.

Industry value was mostly the value of tangible assets in previous industrial period but currently, intangible assets such as brand, technology, know－how, manpower and industry culture decides the competitiveness of industries.

Also, in terms of profit and loss formation of hotel Food and Beverage (F&B) facilities, sales is continuously decreasing and sales cost is increasing. This results as reducement in total sales profit, sales management expense, operating profit, expense besides operation and marketing profit.

When this situation is explained in full detail, customers are reduced and increase in labor and material cost can be seen as the main reason. In this situation, importance of financial management is increasing in hotel industry facilities and evaluating the economical efficiency value of industry is particularly important for financial management.

To date, the most broadly used company evaluation tool is DCF(Discounted Cash Flow).

The purpose of this study is to verify the value of the companies related with F&B and to provide administrative works of hotel managem ent. Recently as food service companies are branching out actively, the distinction between hotel food and beverage service and food service is pointed out and change of management strategy is getting more important. And also, Food service industry is growing at the rate of more than 10% per a year, the sales scale reaching up to 60 trillion won.[1]

Due to this current situation, the hotel food and beverage service has to

---

1) Ki Young Kim and 2 others, *Foodservice Management*, Hyun Hak Sa, 2003, p.104.

be change to new paradigm.

In the developed countries in food service area, such as USA and Japan, family restaurants already take the most primary roles in food service industry.

As yet, Korean companies have focused on external accomplishment rather than increasing profitability. At the same time, not only Korean hotel places of business do not establish logical evaluation models but also practical study of domestic hotel business value evaluation still remain on the primary stage.

Study of value evaluation regarding hotel F&B service by DCF model will provide help for rearing sound hotel F&B service, appropriate judgement of future value for F&B service, adequate investment plan, new F&B service operation strategy and innovative change in F&B service environment.

2) Purpose of the Study

Domestic hotel companies are very unstable. Especially, as researching profitability in food and beverage places of business, most of them have hard time to make proper benefit and sometimes some of them do not receive any benefits at all.[2] As grasping flow of business and situation about profit and loss in food and beverage places of business, unprofitable business places have to be closed so that it gives chances to develop the new trendy business places.

Evaluation of currently operating F&B facility is not being carried out and evaluation is only dependent on income statement.

Especially, evaluating F&B facility by the increase value compared to the

---

2) Seung Woo Baek, *Comparative analysis of managing achievements between chain hotel and domestic hotel*, Konkuk University, 2006, p.97.

previous year is very rudimentary and there is a risk for bankruptcy as evaluation reliability is very low.

〈Table 1-1〉 Comparison of company evaluation method regarding DCF, ROV, EVA and income statement

Classification	DCF	ROV	EVA	Income Statement
Method	Traditional account system DCF+NPV	Black-Scholes Model	Stern Stewart & Co	
Applied firms	* Manufacturing Industry. * Listed Firms. * Unlisted Firms.	* Venture Business.	* Listed Firms. * Insolvent Firms.	* All Firms.
Advantages	* Prediction of Future Condition. * Estimation of change in future cash flow due to business operations. * Excellent in analyzing cash flow compared to other methods. * Most often used in actual business. * Most appropriate for estimating future firm value.	* Analyze of total stock exchange. * Evaluation of option values. * Forces manager to secure diversity. * Increases strategic investment value. * Creating value of uncertainty.	* Predicts stock prices. * Finds insolvent firms in the bond market. * When calculating added value earned from invested capital, the method recognize profit exceeding the amount of own capital and borrowed capital cost as the firm's added values for sales and therefore, the analysis can be focused on profit exceeding own capital.	* Shows the level of creating added value. * Shows the size of added values and operating incomes by viewing manufacturing and sales as same. * Shows profit return information to creditors and stock holders.
Weak Points	* Setting future safeness as premise for decision making makes difficult to decide future measures.	* Researcher's subjective decision. * Difficult to trust market value.	* Depends on short term results. * Does not reflect time value.	* Only shows profit on the accrual basis. * Difficult to predict future economic condition.

※ Written by researcher

When comparing each evaluating method in <Table 1 − 1>, evaluation using DCF model is most favorable. Especially, advantage of value evaluation using DCF model is that prediction of future situation is accurate and based on this, administration manager can establish future management method and strategy plan more easily. However, predicting future situation of F&B facility by Real Option Value(ROV) and Economic Value Added(EVA) model is difficult and these methods have disadvantages of limitation for measuring researcher's subjective judgement and short − term outcomes which results as low reliability for prediction of future status.

Also, prediction of the future is difficult through evaluation that is only dependent on income statement and this method is inadequate for evaluating businesses.

Therefore, using DCF model, this study suggests necessary methods for future management strategy and operation strategy of F&B facilities by accurate prediction of value evaluation regarding hotel F&B facility.

Concrete aim for this study is as followed. Firstly, examining the theory frame of DCF analysis method among hotel related company value evaluation method of advanced countries; secondly, verifying whether the DCF model is rational and systemic value evaluating method for domestic hotel companies with suitable hotel F&B management strategy of our country; and thirdly, comparing basic business evaluating method of current hotel − related business with evaluating method through DCF model for accurate quantitative judgement regarding the adequate value evaluation method of F&B facilities.

Aim of this study is calculating the value by DCF model that has been applied for general manufacturing companies and applying it in management strategy of hotel F&B related facilities, calculating DCF value based on financial statement, income statement and cash flow statement used in hotel companies and using this value, accurately analyzing F&B facilities of hotel company to predict future profit using the most universal method for working out the profit value. The main aim is to suggest the significance and possibility of practical application of study results and direction for future studies.

2　Method and Structure of the Study

1) Method of the Study

This study is made through research literature, internal and external references and data, company value evaluation theories and, research papers about company value evaluation of hotels and companies related with hotels and etc. And also, as using DCF model, we collect Financial Statement of A hotel and B hotel, and Income Statement of food and beverage. In addition, as selecting 14 business places in A hotel, and 7 business places in B hotel in Seoul for empirical analysis.

Based on the main financial statement and the market data from 2001.01 to 2007.12, the subjected hotels are selected and analyzed.

Company value of hotels was applied adequately for domestic situation based on DCF model and it was calculated, analyzed also by using DCF model. Also, analysis subjected companies were limited to currently operating F&B facilities and value of hotel F&B facilities was evaluated for comparative analysis regarding 2 hotels that are operating F&B facilities, other facilities and banquet hall.

This study comparatively analyzed asset and future value of F&B facilities through observation status and formation of domestic hotel industry.

2) Structure of the Study

Chapter 1 is the introduction part to state the problems, purposes, methods and structure of this study.

Chapter 2 is the statement part to explain the concept of business value as the theoretical background of company value evaluation and company value evaluation model. And also, foreign and domestic studies are considered.

Chapter 3 addresses the data collection, the analysis method, and the study model of Korean hotel companies.

Chapter 4 analyzes business value using Discounted Cash Flow and Hamada model, the evaluation model for this study. Also, to perform comparative evaluation of model value and future value, business value was evaluated by classifying as sample hotel F&B facility. Lastly, Net Present Value(NPV) and future estimated profit rate of sample hotel businesses were comparatively evaluated.

Chapter 5 is the conclusion part to summarize the result of this study. Suggestion and limitation of this study and future study plan are addressed.

Chapter 02 Theoretical Background of Business Value

1. Concept of Business Value
2. Evaluation Model of Business Value
3. Previous Studies

Valuation of hotel – Food & Beverage department –

Theoretical Background of Business Value

1 Concept of Business Value

1) Meaning and of Business Value

Generally speaking, there is not only one kind of a value. A value can be defined by different situations. And also, business value can be determined by flow of cash which can be made by companies.[3] In other words, there are various definitions of value. Therefore, according to the purpose of evaluation, the evaluator has to determine the most appropriate definition of value, and there is not only one value for all kinds of evaluation purposes.

The fundamental reason why it is not possible to produce an useful value is based on an inappropriate evaluation method.[4]

In addition, it is essential to apply an appropriate method in order to ob-

---

3) Moon Sung Kim, *Traditional WACC, Miles – Ezzel model and value evaluation of listed enterprises using APV*, Kyung Hee University, 2003, p.4.

4) Jae Ok Kim, *A Study on Reasonable valuation of Venture Company by ROV*, Ho Seo Univ. Ph.D Dissertation, 2002, p.8.

tain the result of useful value evaluation as understanding the object of evaluate and define proper concept of a value.[5]

(1) Meaning of Business Value

There are four meanings of Business Value such as Value as a going concern, Value as an orderly disposition, Value as an orderly disposition, and Value as a forced liquidation.

Business value can be divided by value of company's essence Value of the firm and market value in order to evaluate it. Fair value can be divided by Income value and Asset-based value. Income value is classified as Discount cash flow method model, Dividends valuation model, Earnings valuation, Economic value added model, Excess earnings valuation model and also, Asset-based value is classified as Book value and Liquidation value.

At the same time, the two methods of market value evaluation are Market multiples and Relative value, and Relative value can be classified as Price earnings ratio, Price sales ratio, Price book-value ratio to evaluate business value.

(2) Classification of Business Value

Standards of value based on evaluation objects can be classified as four of them such as Fair Market Value, Investment Value, Insurance Fundamental Value, and Fair Value.[6]

First of all, Fair Market Value means that the price that an interested but no desperate buyer would be willing to pay and an interested but not desperate seller would be willing to accept on the open market. Second,

5) S. P. Pratt and R. F. Reilly and R. P Schweihs, *A Business 3rd Ed,* Irwin, 1996, p.29.
6) *The definition mostly used for FMV in the U.S.* Internal Revenue Service, pp.59-60.

Investment Value means that the estimate value of a certain real estate investment for a particular individual or institutional investor. It is usually separated from fair and general market value. Third, Insurance fundamental value means that the actual value of a company which is based on an underlying perception of its true value as the company runs cash will flow in. Fourth, Fair Value means unbiased estimate of a company.

2) Classification of Business Value Access Method

Business Value Access Method is classified into four different kinds such as Contingent Claim Approach. Income Approach Asset-based Approach, Market Approach.

(1) Contingent Claim Approach

Option is the right to sell or buy assets during certain period of time at a fixed price and certain amount of quantity. And also option is not an obligation but a proper right, so a right can be renounced or exercised according to various conditions. This concept can be applied for company value evaluation. There are two methods which can apply Contingent Claim Approach such as OPM(Option Pricing Model) and ROV.

(2) Income Approach

It is essential for Income Approach to need option that the evaluated company continues to run its business. Business of going concern will create continuous net return and we can estimate the amount of it. As considering risk of the company, Discount rate applies ti estimated amount of net return and the current value is calculated from it. This method is called

Income Approach.

However, while the examiner is estimating the risk of the company, subjectivity of the examiner can be reflected. It means that it is difficult to ensure objectivity. And also, it still matters to decide pertinent point of time to estimate future revenue. There are several methods as using Income Approach such as Discounted Economic Interest, Discounted Cash Flow, Free Cash Flow, Economic Value Added, Leveraged Buy－out Analysis, and Dividend Discount Analysis.[7]

(3) Asset－based Approach

Asset－based Approach is the method to evaluate business by subtracting total liabilities from present total assets from an absolute viewpoint. In this method, asset value is a very significant factor, and it alters greatly according to the definition of the value, that is, either as a liquidation company or as a going concern. At the same time, According to the purpose of the evaluation and subjectivity of the evaluator, the value of evaluation can be different, so in the viewpoint of the valid evaluation it is impossible to determine standard of objective validity. On the other hands, if liquidation company is evaluated to protect bond holder, it would produce the lowest evaluation price so that it could be objective. There are three methods which are used for Asset－Based Approach such as Net Asset Value Method,[8] Replacement Value Method,[9] Liquidation Value Method.[10]

---

7) Sung Su Seol, *A Theoretical Framework for the Valuation of Technology*, Korea Technology Innovation Society, 2000. 3－1. p.11.

8) It is a method evaluate business value with net asset value obtained by subtracting total liabilities from total assets.

9) It is a method to evaluated business value through comparing the value to stock price of a company with similar market price.

10) It is a method to evaluate business based on assets and liabilities of a company.

(4) Market Approach

Relative Price Approach as considering standard companies which has similar conditions is also called Market Approach. This approach evaluates companies as analyzing affine transaction of the comparable company. As using this method, it is possible to predict stock price of growing non−listed company. At the same time, if it is difficult to find comparable company or the company is chose, it can be a problem for evaluator to be subjective. Additionally, in case company chosen for affinity has distorted market price, the evaluated company also could have such price. There are two methods for appling Market Approach such as Comparable Company Analysis and Comparable Transactions Analysis.[11]

2 Evaluation Model of Business Value

1) Traditional Valuation Model

(1) DCF: Discounted Cash Flow[12]

All the amount of asset value can be calculated by all the predictable future cash flow based on the current asset of which method is used the most widely. Business Value can be gained by measuring added value. In order to calculate added value, the amount of cash which is resulted by subtracting outflow from inflow is needed. If a certain standard were established to measure cash flow, it would not be so difficult to measure cash

---

11) Chan Il Kim, *Newest Company Valuation*, Kyung Moon Sa, 2005, p.15.
12) Methods related to DCF are introduced by Modigliani and Miller(1963), Damodaran(1994), Harris and Pringle(1985), Myers(1985), Myers(1974), Miles and Ezzell(1980).

flow by using financial statements of recent 3 years. However, due to the fact that measuring future cash flow involves various reasonable assumptions, it is impossible to obtain exact future cash flow price. Still and all, approximate business can be obtained by making feasible assumption to measure future cash flow price.

Discounted Cash Flow Model would be established as follows if the course of decision making related to future cash inflow and out flow did not alter from current state.

$$Business\ Value = \sum_{t=}^{2} \frac{CF_t}{(1+WACC)}$$

$CF_t = Future\ Cash\ Flow\ expected\ at\ T\ time\ period$

$WACC = Weighted\ Average\ Cost\ of\ Capital$

The formula above can explain that Business Value is current value earned by discounting the total of cash flow gained during presumption period as the company destroys its asset. Discount rate in this formula uses weighted average cost of capital which is earned through weighted average of cost of equity capital and cost of borrowed capital.

In the case of a company with minus($-$) net profit and cash flow due to financial crisis and depression, it is impossible to apply this formula.[13]

Additionally, if a company were under restructuring, it would be not applied because the future of this company is not certain. At the same time, a company which owns intangible asset such as patent rights can not be applied by this formula as a patent right can not produce at present cash flow but it will produce profits in near future. Therefore, in the case of a

---

13) Tom Copeland, Tim Koller, and Jack Muurrin, Dong Won Park, Kwang Jun Kim, Soon Poong Park, *Business Valuation*, Kyung Moon Sa, 2005, p.380.

patent right, it is necessary to evaluate it separately and add the future total. Likewise, the value applying discounted cash flow method does not reflect non－current asset which creates any cash flow. In this case, it is essential to predict the future value separately. Therefore, it has to be applied it in a separate way.

In actual business, Adjusted Discount Cash Flow model is used rather than Discount Cash Flow Model. Adjusted Cash Flow model is a modified version from basic Discount Cash flow model. It presumes cash flow of a company during presumption hence, and then it presumes the value of remaining time for the company, and consequently, concerts all the value in the current business value. When Adjusted Discounted Cash Flow model recognizes, it considers reinvestment of a company to grow constantly and it This method is one of the traditional ways to evaluate company. The formula to calculate Discounted Cash Flow of a year is as follows.

$$CF_t = EBIT_t{}^{14)} \times (1-T) + DEPR_t - CAPEX - NWC + Other_t$$

$CF = Cash\ flow.$　　　　$T = the\ Coporation\ Tax\ rate.$
$DEPR = the\ Depreciation\ Expense.$
$CAPEX = Capital\ Expenditure.$
$Other = Unpaid\ expense. NWC = Net\ Working\ Capital.$

Under the assumption that the company progresses into Steady Period and grows up to g percent(%) which is measured per every year after the predictable period, the value at the end of the period is gained by the perpetuity formula of cash flow given below:

$$TV = [\ CF \times (\ 1+g\ )]\ /\ (\ r-g\ )$$

14) Earning before interest and taxes.

TV = End of term value. r = Discount rate. g = Growth rate.

Therefore, the current business value is the total sum of the discounted current value of annual cash flow during the presumption period and the sum of current value of remaining period value.[15]

$$V = \sum_{t=1}^{n\Leftarrow} \frac{CF}{(1+r)^t} + \frac{TV}{(1+r)^n}$$

In this case, discounted rate is applied by Weighted Average Cost of Capital(WACC) so that cash flow is approached to the aspect of asset. The most important general principle to obtain WACC is to maintain coherence of valuation method and definition of discounted cash flow. In this case, composition rate of capital procurement is acquired through the sum of multiplied return rate and liabilities retrench corporation tax. Therefore these must be reflected to get WACC.

If company procures capital with common stock and liabilities, discount rate is obtained by the method given below.[16]

$$r = \frac{E}{V} r_e + (1-T) \frac{D}{V} r_d$$

r_e = *Cost of equity.*

r_d = *Cost of debt.*

T = *Corporate Tax Rate.*

$\dfrac{E}{V}$ = *A ratio comparing the company's equity to the company's total value.*

---

15) Jae Kyung Lee, *A Study on Deciding Value Factor of Korean E−Business Company,* Kyung Hee Univ. Ph.D Thesis, 2001, p.23.

16) Dong Hwan Kim, Jae Ki Lee, *Modern Business Management Analysis,* Doo Nam Sa, 2000, p.240.

$$\frac{D}{V} = A \ ratio \ comparing \ the \ company's \ debt \ to \ the$$

company's total value.

Return rate of liability is the expected return rate of investors who have stock determined at the minute of procurement. Demand return rate of stock holder is not determined price. Therefore, demand return rate of stock holder need to be calculated through Capital Asset Price Model.

$$r_e = r + \ \times \ (RM - r)$$

$r_f = Risk \ free \ rate \ (National \ Bond \ Return \ Rate).$

$RM = Expected \ market \ return, = Beta \ of \ the \ security.$[17]

And also, Cash Flow model depends on uncertain prediction. However, as a matter of fact, in any kinds of situations, it can work even if the company which is going to be evaluated, there are no comparable companies.[18]

(2) FCF: Free Cash Flow Model

Free Cash Flow Model is one of the company evaluation models that measures the cash company can generate as operating cash flow. It stands the question of by what method will it use to measure the cash which a company can generate, i.e., how it will find the cash. Free Cash Flow is the sum of the net income and the depreciation reduces capital expenditures.[19] To subtract capital expenditures is to make the company to

---

17) RM: Return on a stock or return on Market Portfolio. It shows how the return is affected by the movement of whole stock market. For example, if market(Total Index) increase by 10% and my stock increases by 5% then the beta value is 0.5. That is, if beta becomes 1 then the return moves with the market completely.

18) Bradford Comell, *Corporate Valuation*, IrWin, 1993, pp.83 – 84.

19) S. P. Pratt Shannon and Robert F. Reilly and Robert P. Schweihs, *op. cit.* p.242.

exist as a going concern. Also, subtracting capital expenditures means that company is able to generate it after the presumption period. Financial statements do not affect Free Cash Flow Model when it is calculated before the capital procurement. Free Cash Flow is added on value of remaining period to measure the value of the company. Free Cash Flow Model needs FCF, FCF discounted rate, and growth rate for the application. The past data and financial statement change are considered as predict growth rate.

As mentioned above, WACC is used for the discount rate as in Discounted Cash Flow because FCF is asset based approach. Measurement of Free Cash Flow Model is practiced as follows and it is similar with Discounted Cash Flow:[20]

$$FCF = ERIT(\ 1 - T\ ) + Depreciation - Capital\ expenditure$$
$$-\ Changes\ in\ the\ working\ Capital.$$

Therefore, a company with cash flow growing in safe growth rate is measured by model given as follows:

$$Business\ Value = \sum_{t=1}^{\infty} \frac{FcF_t}{(1 + WACC)}$$

$FCF_t = FCF\ of\ year\ t,$

$WACC:\ Weighted\ Average\ Cost\ of\ Capital.$

And also, after high growth for some time to reach steady growth period, the model can be changed to given below:

---

20) Hyo Suk Kang, Won Heum Lee, Jang Yeon Cho, *Business Valuation*, Hong Moon Sa, 2005, p.130.

$$Business\ Value = \sum_{t=1}^{n} \frac{FCF_t}{(1+WACC)^t} + \frac{FCF_{n+1}/(WACC_n - g_n)}{(1+WACC)^n}$$

WACC: weighted average cost of capital of during high growth period.

WACC^n : weighted average cost of capital of steady growth period.

g^n : constant growth rate in steady growth period.

First is the current value of discounted free cash flow of presumption period.

Second is the current value of discounted value of remaining period.

FCFn+1 is gained by multiplying growth rate of steady growth period with free cash flow of the last year of presumption period.

(3) Free Cash Flows to Equity Discount Models

① Steady growth FCFE Model

Steady growth Free Cash Flow for Equity Discount model determines the value of a company growing in steady growth rate.

The value of stock is determined by expected FCFE, steady growth rate and cost of equity capital.[21]

$$P_0 = \frac{FCFE_1}{r - g_n}$$

p0: Value of Stock today.

FCFE1: expected FCFE in the next period.

---

21) Aswath, *Investment Valuation; Tools and Techniques for Determining the Value of any Asset,* John Wiley&Sons, Inc, pp.219 − 234.

r: cost of equity capital.

gn: FCFE perpetual growth rate.

② High Growth Period Model

Value of Stock is gained by adding the discounted current value of FCFE per every year with current value of presumed stock price at the end of the high growth period.

Value of Stock = Current value of FCFE + Current value of stock price at the end of high growth period.

$$= \sum_{t=1}^{n} \frac{FCFE_t}{(1+r)^t} + \frac{P_n}{(1+r)^n}$$

FCFEt: FCFE in year t.

Pn: Stock price at the end of high growth.

r: Required rate of return of capital investment

in high growth period.

Stock price at the end of rapid growth is obtained by perpetual growth model.

Pn = FCFEn + 1/(rn − gn)

gn: Growth rate after high growth period.

rn: Required rate of return of capital investment in steady growth period.

③ E − model

In E model, the current value is calculated by the current value of expected FCFE over all these three stages of growth.

$$P_0 = \sum_{t=1}^{n1} \frac{FCFE}{(1+r)^t} + \sum_{t=n1=1}^{n2} \frac{FCFE_t}{(1+r)^t} + \frac{P_{n2}}{(1+r)^{n2}}$$

P0: Value of Stock today.

FCFEt: FCFE in year t.

r: cost of capital.

Pn2: Terminal price at the end of transitional period $= FCFE_{r2+2/(r-g)_n}$

n1: End of initial high growth period.

n2 = End of transition period.

Difference between Dividend Discount Model and FCFE Model is the definition of cash flow. While FCFE Model defines it as free cash flow for every financial obligation and investment fund as wide meaning. Dividend Discount Model is defined as expected dividend of stock for stock holder as narrow meaning, FCFE model provides more value when evaluating a company subject for acquisition or a company which seized an opportunity to superintend a company.[22]

(4) Free Cash Flows to Firm

① Steady State FCFE Model

Companies that have cash flow growth in steady growth rate could be evaluated by steady state FCFE model. These companies use the model as follows:[23]

Business Value $= FCFE1/(WACC - gn)$

FCFE1: expected FCFE in next year.

---

22) Yoon Ho Lee, *A Study on Valuation of Food Service related Company, ROV and DCF model of Listed Company*, Kyonggi University, 2007, pp.12 – 14.

23) Han Kyu Jung, Chul Jung Kim, Pyeong Sik Yoon, *Valuation*, Kyung Moon Sa, 2002, p.329.

WACC: cost of capital.

gn: FCFE perpetual growth rate.

$$\text{or Business Value} = \sum_{t=1}^{00} \frac{FCFF}{(1+WACC)^t}$$

FCFEt: FCFE in year t.

WACC: cost of capital.

if a company reaches steady state in n years business value is:

$$\text{Business Value} = \sum_{t=1}^{n} \frac{FCFF}{(1+WACC)^t} + \frac{FCFF_{n=1}/(WACC_{N-g_n})}{(1+WACC)^n}$$

WACC = cost of capital in high growth period.

WACCn = cost of capital in steady growth period.

gn: constant growth rate in steady growth period.

It is essential to consider the method for calculating business value by reducing Free Cash Flows to Firm with cost of capital. The Value of equity is gained through subtracting market value of liability from business value. FCFE become cash flow before interests are paid, so FCFE model is suitable for a company which has high leverage or changes, periodically.

(5) Dividend Discount Model

Investors expect cash flow of the general form when they purchase stocks. In other words, it is dividend of holding period of stocks and expected stock price at the end of the period. Expected price at the end of the period is determined by future dividend after the period. Therefore, the value of stock is the current value of future dividends paid forever.[24]

$$Value\ of\ Stock = \sum_{t=1}^{n} \frac{DPS_t}{(1+r)^t}$$

DPSt: Expected Cash Dividend per stock.

r: return of stock(cost of capital).

The logical basis of this model is that the value of company asset that is the value of present company discounted by appropriated discount rate of the future cash flow of the company asset.

Proper discount rate is the discount rate in which risk of the future cash is reflected.

Therefore, Fundamental methods of using this model are expected dividend method and return of equity method.

Expected growth rate of net profit and payout ratio process is needed for gaining expected dividend method. Return of equity or return of stock is determined by risk of stock. Risk of stock, thus, is measured in different ways by models respectively. Capital Asset Pricing Model is measured by market β and Arbitrate Pricing Model is measured by element β. Dividend Discount Model has flexibility to consider discounted rate occurred by changing in market interest rate and risk. There are a range models which used for evaluating companies in terms of growth rate of company following.

① Gordon Growth Model

Gordon Growth Model is used for evaluating companies which have dividends to grow at a constant rate.

---

24) J. Williams, The Theory of Investment Value, Cambridge MA: *Harvard University press,* 1938.

It is a model to evaluate stocks which is based on expected dividends, return of stock and expected growth rate of the next period.

$$Value\ of\ Stock = \frac{DPS_1}{r-g}$$

DPS1: Expected dividend per share one year from now.

r: required rate of return of stock(cost of capital).

g: Growth rate in dividends forever(assuming it will last forever).

Gordon growth model is a simple and convenient way to evaluate a stock, but it is a very sensitive model to grow rate which is inputted variable.

It is sensitive to economic growth rate as this model is the most appropriate for companies with growth rate similar to economic growth rate or with low growth rate, and with firm dividend policy that will keep up its performance constantly providing dividends stably.

② Growth stage Dividend Discount Model.

Growth stage dividend discount model allows two stages of growth – the one is initial phase where the growth rate is high and another one is subsequent steady state where the growth rate is stable and it is expected to remain so for the long term.

This model assumes that companies will grow in high growth rate for initial n years and then they will grow in stable growth that lasts forever afterwards.

Value of Stock = Current value of Dividends during extraordinary phase +PV of terminal price.

$$P_0 = \sum_{t=1}^{n} \frac{DPS_t}{(1+r)} + \frac{P_n}{(1+r)^n}$$

$$P_n = \frac{DPS}{(r_n - g_n)}$$

DPSt = Expected dividends per share in year t.

r = Cost of equity in high growth period.

Pn = Price at the end of year n.

g = High growth rate for the first n years.

gn = Steady state growth rate forever after year n.

rn = Cost of equity in steady state growth.

If high growth rate(g) and payout ratio are constant for the first n years, this formula can be simplified:

$$P_n = \frac{DPS_t(1+g)\left(1 - \dfrac{(1+g)^n}{(1+r)^n}\right)}{r-g} + \frac{DPS_{n+1}}{(r_n - g_n)(1+r)^n}$$

Growth stage dividend discount model is convenient to evaluate equity and is based on the fact that current value of expected dividend is the value of stock. Even though the model is criticized for limitation in usage surprisingly, the model verified as very effective model for evaluation, which is applied in various situations there are a limitation in usage.

(6) Stock holder cash flow method

① MM Matrix

The MM Matrix(1958) explains the capital structure theory on the assumption of a perfect market. However, in the real world, there are various factors that make the market imperfect. Tax is the most typical example of these factors. From all types of taxes, the MM Matrix(1963) only considers corporation tax and the Miller Matrix(1977) considers both corporation tax and individual income tax. Also, the bankruptcy cost theory of Kraus & Litzenberger(1973) considers bankruptcy cost as a imperfect factors and the Agency Theory of Jensen & Meckling(1976) considers the agency cost due to information asymmetry.

By applying corporation tax as a imperfect factor, the 3 propositions presented by MM in 1958 can be adjusted as follows.

a) First Proposition

When corporation tax exists, the value of indebted firms is larger than non indebted firms with the difference equal to the current value of liabilities tax reduction effects. In other words,

$$V_L = V_U + t.B.$$

b) Second Proposition

K_e increases with the increase of leverage even when corporation tax exists but the increase is slightly slower due to liabilities tax reduction effects.

c) Third Proposition

It is advantageous to raise funds for conducting new investment plans from borrowed capitals.[25]

② The MM Matrix and Hypothesis

The relation between business value and capital structure has been a subject of discussion for a long time between the academic circles and practical

---

25) Eui Kyung Lee, 「Finance management – Theory and application」, Kyung – moon sa 2005, pp.335 – 340.

businesses. The subject is yet most essential for corporate financing. Miller & Modigliani's propositions in the 1950s and the adjusted propositions in the 1960s were the first ever to create a theory for these relations.[26]

In this paper, we will focus on business valuation, capital cost and assumption related with the MM(1963)'s adjusted proposition. The MM adjusted proposition is based on the following assumptions.

First, businesses create debts but do not redeem and continuously use without any time limits.

Second, operation cash flow should be fairly continued and the size must be larger than the size needed for receiving annual tax reductions for interest costs.[27]

The MM adjusted proposition no.1 can be explained as follows.

$$V_L = V_U + t \times B$$

In which, V_L: Value of non indebted firm.

V_U: Value of indebted firm.

t: Corporation Tax.

B: Amount of Debt.

This means that the value of indebted firm is larger than the value of non indebted firm with the difference of leverage profit tB.

The MM adjusted proposition no.2 is drawn from the first and is as follows.

$$K_e^L = K_e^U + (K_e^U - Kd)(1-t)\frac{B}{S}$$

---

26) Moon Sung Kim(2003), *op. cit.* pp.10 − 11.

27) Eui kyung Lee(2005), *op. cit.* pp.389 − 390.

In which, K_e^L*: Cost of Equity of indebted firm.*

K_e^U*: Cost of Equity of non indebted firm.*

Kd: Liabilities Cost.

B/S: Debt Ratio.

t: Corporation Tax.

B: Amount of Debt.

The formula shows that the Cost of Equity K_e^L increases with the use of debts but the range of increase is fluent compared to no corporation tax. For this reason, WACC decreases with the use of debts. According to MM adjusted proposition no.3, it is advantageous to raise funds needed for new investment plans from borrowed capitals. This is because the WACC decreases with the use of debts and if the cash flow of the investment is fixed, smaller WACC means larger investment value.

③ Hamada Model

The Hamada Model shows the relation between the stock beta of indebted firms and non indebted firms and can be explained as follows.

$$\beta_L = \left[1 + (1-t)\frac{B}{S}\right] \cdot \beta_U$$

The stock beta of indebted firms increases along with the increase of financial risk caused by the increase of leverage. This value can be calculated from the stock beta of non indebted firms.

According to MM(1963), when corporation tax exists, the value of indebted firms V_L is larger than the value of non indebted firms V_U with the difference of the current value of interest cost tax reduction because in this case, the interest payments for liabilities are recognized as cost. Therefore, the following formula is created.

$$V_L = V_U + t.B$$

From this formula, the beta of business value is as follows.

$$\beta(V_L) = \frac{V_U}{V_L}.\beta^{U_S} + \frac{t.B}{V_L}.\beta_B$$

On the other hand, business value is always the sum total of equity capital and debt value, therefore, the following formula can be created.

$$V_L = B + S$$

From this formula, the beta of business value is as follows.

$$\beta(V_L) = \frac{B}{V_L}.\beta_B + \frac{B}{V_L}.\beta^{L_S}$$

The beta of business value evaluated from the formulas above were all evaluated from a same firm. Therefore, the values should all be equal and the following formula can be created.[28]

$$\frac{V_L}{V_L}.\beta^{U_S} + \frac{t.B}{V_L}.\beta_B = \frac{S}{V_L}.\beta^{L_S}$$

④ Hamada hypothesis

When calculating the WACC, the stock beta is adjusted to match the debt ratio and for indebted firms, the stock beta increases with the increase

---

28) Eui Kyung Lee(2005), *op. cit.* p.283.

of leverage, which causes financial risk to increase. The Hamada Model shows that the stock beta of indebted firms(β_L) can be calculated from that of non indebted firms(β_v). This is called the Hamada Model and is as follows.

$$\beta_L = \beta_U \left[1 + (1-t) \frac{B}{S} \right]$$

The formula was created from MM(1963) adjusted proposition no.1 and the debt beta β_d is set as 0. Therefore, the Hamada Model is based on the following assumptions.

The debt used by firms is risk free($\beta_d = 0$). Therefore, the firm's capital cost of debts is risk free rate of interest.

This assumption is not included in MM(1963) adjusted proposition. Therefore, the Hamada Model is stricter compared to MM(1963)'s proposition. If the firm's liability is risk free and the liability interest rate is equal to the risk free rate of interest, the WACCs drawn from the MM adjusted proposition and the Hamada Mode are equal, therefore, the same result for both methods.

The firm's liability used in both methods has risk in the real world. Therefore, the capital cost payed for liabilities is higher than the risk free rate of interest and the interest rate differs from firm to firm. Under these conditions the Hamada Model can not be used. This is because the Hamada Model is based on the assumption of risk free liability. Therefore, for these cases, the MM proposition, which doesn't have a risk free assumption, should be used rather than the Hamada Model.

3   Previous Studies

1) Foreign Studies

Ely & Waymire(1999) researched correlation between Intangible Asset and Stock Price with different account treatments respectively. This is the research about Intangible Asset which affects stock price and Intangible Asset which affects future economic profits. In this research, the significant point is that when the Intangible Asset can be measured reliably, it is related with Stock Price directly and ultimately. And also, they researched how closely Stock Price is related to Intangible Asset, and they analyzed whether, when Intangible Asset is separated from Sock Price. it is possible for Stock Price to get lower or not. As a result of this research, investors tended to consider Intangible Asset as a more valuable aspect when the company make more profits. At the same time, Ely & Waymire proved that in the financial statement, to report Intangible Asset and to treat Intangible Asset as a different item are helpful for maintaining and reporting Stock Price. And also, they find that Stock Price does not change at all even if they manipulate account processes of Intangible Asset. However when Intangible Asset is reported separately from other asset items in the financial statement, book value of tangible asset is appeared directly and positively.[29]

Lev and Zarowin(1999) analyzed how different in each companies future economic benefit about research and development expense, uncertainty, and response square of early stock return rate from benefit are. The result of analysis showed that the response square of research and development ex-

---

29) Intangible Assets and Stock Price in the Pre‒SEC Era. *Journal of Accounting Research*, pp.17‒51.

pense, and stock return rate has positive correlation. And also, the response square of future profit and research and development expense is shown as positive correlation. In addition, early stock return rate from benefit shows positively.[30]

Collins, Maydew and Weiss(1997) performed systematic changes in the value‒relevance of earnings and book values over time. The results are as follows. First, contrary to claims in the professional literature, in the professional literature, the combined value‒relevance of earnings and book values has not declined over the past forty years and in fact, appears to have increased slightly. Second, while the incremental value‒relevance of 'bottom line' earnings has declined, it has been replaced by increasing value‒relevance of book value. Third, much of the shift in value‒relevance firm earnings to book values can be explained by the increasing frequency and magnitude of one‒time, the increasing frequency of negative earnings, and changes in average firm size and intangible intensity across time.[31]

Bernard(1995) noted that the Ohlson(1995) and Feltham and Ohlson(1995) studied stand among the most important developments in capital markets research in recent years. The studies provide a foundation for redefining the appropriate objectives of research on the relation between financial statement data and firm value. At the same time, they provide some structure for modeling in a field where structure has been sorely lacking. Fundamental analysis involves a study of a firm's current activities and prospects for purpose of estimating its value.[32]

Burgstahler and Dichev(1997) developed an option‒style model of equity

---

30) Lev, B. and Zarowin. P. The Boundaries of Financial Reporting and How to Extend Them, *Journal of Accounting Research(supplement)* Vol.37, autumn, 1999, pp.353‒385.

31) Collins, D. W., E. Maydew, and I. Weiss, Changes in the Value‒Relevance of Earning and Book Values over the Past Forty Year, *Journal of Accounting and Economics*, Vol.24 Issue 1, 1997, pp.39‒67.

32) Bernard, V, The Feltham‒Ohlson Framework: Implications for Empiricists, *Contemporary Accounting Research*, Vol.11, No.2 Spring, 1995, pp.733‒747.

value that incorporates the capitalized value of the firm's expected earnings(under the assumption that the firm continues its current way of employing resources) but also explicitly recognizes the value of the firm's adaption option(i.e., the value of the option to convert the firm's resources to alternative, more productive uses). The results implied that equity value is a function of both expected earnings to book value in contrast to models which incorporate one or the other, and that the form of the function is convex, in contrast to models which assume the two elements of value are simply additive.[33]

Hayn(1995) hypothesized that because shareholders have a liquidation option, losses are not expected to perpetuate. They are thus less informative than profits about the firm's future prospects. The results are consistent with the hypothesis.[34]

Hand(2000) noted that business can be evaluated through book value and ordinary profit of e-business companies. The research is used business value and ordinary profit indicator as independent variable and market value as dependent variable on regression analysis. The research divided 167 companies into two categories: companies with surplus profit and with deficit profit. Regression of companies with surplus profit significantly resulted R2 reaching 83%.[35]

Amir and Lev(1996) examined the value-relevance to investors of financial(accounting) and intangible information of independent cellula companies and found that on a stand-alone basis, financial information(earnings, book values, and cash flows) were largely irrelevant for security valuation. in-

---

33) Burgstahler, D., and I. Dichev, Earning, Adaptation, and Equity Value, *The Accounting Review-(April)*, 1997, pp.187-216.

34) Hayn, C., The Information Content of Losses, *Journal of Accounting and Economics(september)*: 1995, pp.125-153.

35) Biddle, G., P. Chen and G. Zhang, When Capital Follows Profitability: Non-Linear Residual Income Dynamics, *Review of Accounting Studies*(June/September): 2001, pp.229-265.

tangible indicators, such as POPS(a growth proxy) and market Penetration(an operating performance measure), were highly value−relevant. However, combined with intangible information, earnings do contribute to the explanation of prices.[36]

Zhang examined that the model predicts that equity value increases with earnings for any given book value. On the other hand, given earnings, equity value is expected to increase with book value for low−efficiency firms, be insensitive to book value for steady−state firms, and decrease with book value for growth firms. The valuation function is predicted to be convex in earnings and book value because of the option to expand or contract the operating scale. For firms expected to remain in a steady state, equity value reduces to a linear functions of earnings.[37]

Zhang investigated analyst forecast inefficiency from an information perspective. In This study, we found that analysts appear not to adjust sufficiently away from their prior beliefs and under weight new information in revising their earnings forecasts regardless of whether analysts had a linear or a quadratic loss function. As a result, current forecast errors and subsequent forecast revisions were negative following bad news but positive following good news. The opposite effects of information uncertainty on forecast errors and subsequent forecast revisions following good versus bad news support the analyst under reaction hypothesis.[38]

Hirschey(1982) found that the intangible capital issue is investigated through use of a market valuation model. In this approach, significant future intangible capital effects of advertising and R&D are suggested to the

---

36) Amir, E., and B. LEV, Value−Relevance of intangible Information: The Wireless Communication Industry, *Journal of Accounting & Economics:* 1996, pp.3−30.

37) Zhang, G., Accounting Information, Capital Investment Decisions, and Equity Valuation: Theory and Empirical Implications, *Journal of Accounting Research(Autumn):* 2000, pp.271−295.

38) Zhang, X. F. Information Uncertainty and Analyst Forecast Behavior. *Contemporary Accounting Research* 23(2): 2006, pp.565−590.

extent that current expenditures have significant effects on the market value of the firm. Given positive market value influences, individual coefficient estimates can be used to estimate both the total stock of intangible capital as well as average annual depreciation rate for advertising and R&D.[39]

Schwartz · Moon performed option model to evaluate internet companies based on profit creation and expected growth rate of the cost. The study supplied systematic way to calculate business value as Schwartz · Moon considered internet company value revealed in market of high profit growth rate and conditional coefficient reasonable. They insist that parameter which applies this method is the most important factor for the valuation. To apply this model, various processes need to be exercised, and for reasonable process, knowledge regarding a company and industry is essential. Even though there is the possibility of insolvency, if additional growth rate and volatility during growing period are high, it is concluded that current market price is not abnormally high. However, the study is criticized for using certain and only company(Amazon.com) for parameters and valuating semester data which do not consider the seasonal profit changes.[40]

Rajgopal · Kotha & Venkatachalam stated that there is a relationship between evaluation of the internet company its non−financial informations such as web traffic which can be the variable to explain market value of internet company such as yahoo.com and amazon.com thus, they studied the relationship between statistics and business value under the assumption that financial information can not work as an indicator for evaluation, Web traffic was selected to work as an indicator. These theme were studied. First, it has a value as itself or it is an assumption for company strategies. Second, it has a value for predicting future revenue. Third, it has a value

---

39) Hirschey, M. Intangible Capital Aspects of Advertising and R&D Expenditures, *Journal of Industrial Economics*, NO.1, 1982.

40) E S & M. Schwart, Moon, Rational Pricing of Internet Companies, *Financial Analysts Journal*, No.3, 2000.

of potential relativity created by the network. Rajgopal and 2 others re-searched financial information from financial statement which is submitted to US SEC regarding 92 internet companies of open distribution and ana-lyzed the number of unique visitors and reach rate of web connection data collected by 'PC data', web site evaluation institute.[41]

Venturestorm suggested the evaluation method which vest additional measures to 6 evaluation factors. First is ability of the executive. It means that personality of the executive, faculty of the executive and the board, and the wealth of the executive are evaluated. Second one is technology level which means that maintenance and repair of company's produce are evaluated. Third one is marketability. It means that the survey on the scale of the established market and latent market is valuated. Forth is Financial soundness which means financial statement preparation and future cash analysis are valuated. Fifth one is Economical efficiency which means busi-ness value is analyzed and valuated to examine investment profitability which corresponds to the invested capital. Sixth one is Management envi-ronment which means analyzed how much did the sociocultural, political, science – technological factors effect the growth of the company.[42]

R.G.Mc Grath& I. C. Mac Millan suggested evaluation method which marks the score of the factors which determine the value of the project from Real Option stand – point. Development cost and Commercializing cost subtracted from Expected flow is defined as intrinsic value of the project. The value has high volatility of future revenue and high possibility of maintaining competitive advantage. In case of failure, when the loss is lesser, the value will increase higher. Check list is applied to measure ex-pected cash flow and the cost.[43]

---

41) Rajgopal Shivaram and Suresh kotha and mohan Venkatachalam, *The Relevance of web Traffic for Stock Prices of Internet Firms University Of Washington*, Oct. 2000.
42) www.Venturestorm.com.

Ohlson(1995), Feltham and Ohlson(1995) created a model using accounting information to valuate. The model based on future dividend discount model and supplemented fundamental assumption of accounting structure. First, the model valuates the theoretical validity. Second, the model considers accounting information as the value determining factors by applying accounting numbers directly rather than disassembling the accounting information to obtain the cash flow. Third, the accounting numbers model depends on the attribute of accounting measure. Forth, If the expected value retains total revenue attribute of capitalization after the calculation accounting information for infinity is needless. Fifth, despite the difference of accounting operation of respective companies and arbitrary accounting operation fundamental model for the valuation is maintained. Sixth, even if the investors do not use the accounting information they observe the model beforehand. Hence the fundamental model is maintained whether the accounting information is the information used by the investors.[44]

2) Domestic studies

Choi, Kwon and Lobo(2000) studied the reported value of intangible asset and relation of depreciate expense and company value through positive analysis. They verified the value relation of intangible asset by 'matched pair portfolio analysis' and 'multiple regression analysis.' In portfolio analysis, company market value reflected the value of reported intangible asset. However, noticeable fact is that company value does not have direct value relationship with intangible asset depreciate expense, intangible asset and

---

43) R.G.Mc Grath& I. C. Mac Millan, Assessing Technology Projects Using Real Options Reasoning: The STAR Approach, *Research Technology Management*, July/August, 2000.

44) G. A. Feltham and J. A. Ohlson Valuation and Clean Surplus Accounting for Operations and Financial Activities Contemporary Accounting Research, Vol.11(Spring), 1995, pp.689 – 731.

other categories on balance sheet are not treated differently and it was values were proved to be not measured. Result of regression analysis was same as the result of portfolio analysis. This is not much different from the results of previous studies on value relationship of intangible asset and value non-relationship of intangible asset depreciate expense. Two hypothesis were chosen for this study. First was positive analysis of whether reported amount of intangible asset, value of intangible asset and intangible asset depreciate expense were treated differently with other categories on balance sheet and income statement. Result of positive analysis based on portfolio analysis showed that company value had positive relationship with intangible asset value reported on balance sheet but intangible asset depreciate expense on income sheet did not have strong influence. This means that market value of intangible asset does not have great difference compared to 1 dollar of other categories on balance sheet. Noticeable fact for intangible asset depreciate expense on income statement is that company value is not greatly influenced by intangible asset depreciate expense but intangible asset depreciate expense influences the value of intangible asset and other categories on income statement.[45]

Joon hwan Lee(2001) verified company value relationship of intangible asset using EBO model.[46] Results showed that intangible asset on balance sheet is related to company value and can be chosen as a beneficial variable for explaining company value.[47]

Bong hee Han(1998), setting domestic companies as the subject, verified whether profit usefulness decreases by various problems related to accounting profit measurement regarding specific company, industry due to rapidly

---

45) Choi, W., S. Kwon., and J. Lobo, Market Valuation of Intangible Assets, *Journal of Business Research* 49, 1996, pp.34 - 45.

46) Edwards and Bell(1961), Excess profit model of Ohlson(1995) and others.

47) Joon Hwan Lee, *Value relationship of intangible asset data*, Kyung Hee University, 2001, p.84.

changing industrialization under current company accounting standard. In other words, among overall company asset, intangible asset is increasing due to industrial development such as expansion and mechanization but intangible asset is not appropriately evaluated nor documented as current domestic company accounting standard chooses historical cost valuation basis. Under this hypothesis, study on the decrease of accounting profit usefulness of domestic capital market was performed based on Francis and Schipper(1996) study model. Under the hypothesis that historical cost valuation basis for profit measurement used in current company accounting standard is inappropriate for high－tech companies, sample companies were divided into high－tech and low－tech companies to observe the decrease rate of explanation ability(Adj. R^2) for each year.[48] Results showed that decrease of accounting profit usefulness did not deepen due to the fact that company accounting standard is inappropriate for high－tech companies.

Hye young Jung(1995), by using Ohlson evaluation model, suggested and positively analyzed a model for company value that expresses accounting values on balance sheet such as net property book value, future cash flow, future growth rate, company risk and conservative degree of accounting method in function. Results showed that in PBR determinant analysis, the ratio of PBR book value, future ordinary profit among various future cash flow variables showed the highest correlations with PBR. Among PBR determinants that consider PBR future cash flow, future growth rate, company risk and accounting method, presumptive coefficient of variables other than company risk and accounting method was proved significant. Also, in stock price determinant analysis, regression analysis was progressed for net property book value, future cash flow, future growth rate, company risk, accounting method and current stock price index. Results showed that rele-

---

48) Bong Hee Han, Positive study on the possibility of usefulness increase for financial profit data in domestic capital market 『Accounting study』(No.9), 1998, p.22.

vance of overall model was significant and explanation ability of model was also very high. Therefore, it was proved that net property book value has great affect on determining company value.[49]

Joung chun Lee, and Woong rak Oh(2004) applied Ohlson model that evaluates company value by accounting variables and option model in evaluating company value for KOSDAQ general company and venture company which have different company characteristics. They positively verified whether relevance of company value evaluation model can be different according to company characteristic. Results showed that general companies did not have difference in relevance of company value evaluation between Ohlson model and option model. New profit model was more relevant than Ohlson model for value evaluation of venture companies. Also, general company and venture company with different characteristics had great difference in Ohlson model coefficient and explaining ability. This indicates that when evaluating company value by Ohlson model, the characteristic of company should be considered and suggests that studies related to company value by Ohlson model should have controlled company characteristic.[50]

Chu ran Jung(2003) verified whether explaining ability of company value increases if book value and net profit is modified by considering research development investment and advertisement expense as surrogates for intangible asset compared to the original data. Also, by including non−financial data other than financial data, they verified whether explaining ability of company value increases additionally. Results showed that non−financial data such as diversification degree, market share, appreciation stock potion granting rate, pay of executives, percentage of share for insiders in KOSDAQ companies had

---

49) Hye Young Jung, Price determining model by accounting value, 「Accounting study」(20；1), 1995, pp.1−27.

50) Joung Chun Lee and Woong Rack Oh, Study on the difference of relevance in company value evaluation model according to company characteristic: Focusing on KOSDAQ regular companies and venture companies, 「Accounting study」(29；2): 2004, pp.157−185.

additional company value explaining ability.[51]

Moon chul Kim(1994) discussed the role of accounting data in company value evaluation from the standpoint of determining issue price of IPO and analyzed the difference of accounting data roles between main company characteristics. From the study based on the model of considering not profit and net book value as company value demonstrated variable, these variables were found to be significant demonstrated variable for issue price of IPO. Especially, explaining ability for accounting data of company value increased as age of company was older. Usefulness of accounting data was higher in high－tech industries compared to general industries. This study indicates that net profit and net book value is a relevant demonstrated variable of company value.[52]

Seung myo Shin(1995) analyzed based on Ohlson's company value evaluation model under the hypothesis that accounting data is a useful variable for predicting stock price. He suggested that it is an demonstrated variable that presumably can explain the stock price and current book value may be useful for planning investment strategy. He verified by using variables such as current profit, essential profit presumed by beta and future expectation profit presumed by the profitability tendency from past to present. Sample companies were controlled according to asset revaluation period and demonstrated variable used for evaluation was standardized between each company to achieve periodical sameness. Results indicated that variables significantly explained the issue price for accounting years that were analyzed.[53]

Hyae Young Jung, Hyun Lee and Sang ki Chang(1995) induced a model

---

51) Chu Ran Jung, *Study on value revaluation of Korean KOSDAQ enterprises － role of non － linear model and non － financial data*, Kyung Hee University, 2003, pp.2 － 3.

52) Moon Chul Kim, Role of accounting data on the issue price of newly subscribed stock, 「Accounting study」, No.19, 1994, pp.73 － 100.

53) Seung Myo Shin, *Valuation of stock price using accounting data*, Seoul University, 1995, pp.29 － 38.

that determines net book value, future cash flow, future growth rate and discount rate on balance sheet as functions for financial statement analysis and investment strategy by company intrinsic value determination. They analyzed stock price using PBR. PBR showed the highest correlation with the flow of future ordinary profit. Also, future study project for accounting is researching about whether outcome of value evaluation model changes according to the accounting method used in company. In other words, they will study about outcome difference of model according to the conservative degree for accounting method.[54]

Moon hyun Kim(1998) studied the relationship between conservative accounting degree and company characteristic variable by using accounting data. Results for the influence of company characteristic variable on company value proved that company scale(total asset) variable had negative ($-$) relationship with conservatism, and debt ratio and percentage of share within minority shareholders rate had positive ($+$) relationship.[55]

Choong ryul Yoo(1999) adapted domestic capital market in company value evaluation and studied the value relationship difference of profit and book value, two important value evaluation variable, according to the company characteristic. Ohlson model was applied after classifying the company characteristic by profitability, growth and technique. Results showed that even the book value which has a low value explaining ability compared to the profit, when used while considering company characteristic variables expressed as profitability and growth, sometimes may have higher explaining ability than profit. He discovered that explaining ability of total model can be elevated. Also, when growth variable is added in case of equal profit-

---

54) Hyae Young Jung, Hyun Lee, Sang Ki Chang, Financial statement analysis and investment strategy according to company's intrinsic value determination, 「Accounting study」, 20; 1, 1995, pp.101－130.

55) Moon Hyun Kim, *Influence of company characteristic on company value evaluation using accounting data*, Seoul University, 1998, pp.8－24.

ability, predicting ability of future expected profit was increased.[56]

For studying the relationship of financial characteristic and accounting policy in companies, Young do Kwon(1991) set a hypothesis and progressed unfavorite and multivariate analysis to verify whether there is a difference of financial characteristic variable between companies with long term application of different accounting method and to see if the different variable influences selecting accounting method. Independent variable was set as debt ration, current ratio, depreciative asset ratio and tangible fixed asset ratio, based on contract process theory. Scale and tax rate was set based on politic process theory. Accounting policy which is a dependent variable was set based on depreciation method and inventory asset evaluation method. Results showed that inventory asset evaluation method rejected the hypothesis and depreciation method selected the debt ratio(total debt/total asset) hypothesis.[57]

In soon Lee(1994) analyzed the relationship of accounting method and company characteristic to verify the selecting motive of company's accounting policy. Company characteristic variables were debt ratio, current ratio, company scale(larger number of sales amount), growth, market share, equipment investment increase rate, concentration of asset, tax rate and reserve ratio. Accounting method for increasing the reporting profit was used as financial cost allotment, market share and equipment investment increase rate is higher and scale is bigger.[58]

Jung ho Choi(1994) positively analyzed the influence of research development and advertisement expense on company value by Q of Tobin, focus-

---

56) Choon Ryul Yoo, *Study on value relation of variables for company value evaluation according to company characteristic,* Seoul University, 1999, pp.49 – 51.

57) Young Do Kwon, *Influence of company financial characteristic on accounting regulation – Focusing on depreciation method and inventory asset evaluation method,* Kyungbuk University, 1991, pp.99 – 102.

58) In Soon Lee, *Study on selecting motive of accounting regulation within managers,* Youngnam University, 1994, pp.97 – 100.

ing on manufacturing industry among domestic listed enterprises. Results of analysis is as followed.

Firstly, advertisement expense does not contribute in increasing the company value of the current year.

Secondly, ordinary research development expense also does not contribute in increasing the company value of the current year.

Thirdly, unordinary research development expense had positive affects on company value through the entire investigation period. Therefore it was proved that accounting method that appropriated as asset and depreciate during the period of efficacy was relevant.

Fourthly, when ordinary and unordinary research development expense is both included in the analysis, it was proved to have positive affects on company value.

Fifthly, presumptive coefficient of controlled variables included in the model other than market risk showed positive ($+$) value and was found to be significant which proved to be an important demonstrated variable of Tobin Q.[59]

Myung jang Baek(1994) positively analyzed the influence of company's research development expense on profit, sales and stock price for 114 manufacturing industries form 1980 to 1993. Ordinary profit increase rate or regulated ordinary profit increase rate of the research year was used for dependent variable, research development expense intensity for independent variable and profit increase rate with advertisement expense intensity of industry that the sample company is included for controlled variable. Regulated ordinary profit is the sum of ordinary profit and research development expense which is the possibly obtained ordinary profit if research development expense had not been spent. Intensity of research development ex-

---

59) Jung Ho Choi, *Influence of advertisement expense and research development expense on company value: Positive analysis by Tobin Q,* 『Accounting study』, No.19, 1994, pp.103 - 124.

pense used the added amount of marketed research development expense and research development expense on manufacturing cost specification at t period deferred research development expense compared to sales amount Accumulated research development expense intensity is the research development expense compared to the sales amount during $(1+i)$ period and advertisement expense intensity is advertisement expense divided by the sales amount. Results showed that profit increase rate of researched year and research development expense intensity of previous 5 years(research development expense/sales amount) had a positive $(+)$ correlation and the influence was greatest before 3 years but all was not statistically significant. Advertisement expense intensity of researched year and ordinary profit rate had a negative $(-)$ correlation. Also, regression analysis of dependent variable as accumulated excess stock profit rate of 12 months and independent variable as non-expected research development expense expressed a positive sign but was not significant. Non-expected advertisement expense expressed a positive sign partially and was significant and not significant. However, before 1987 expressed a negative $(-)$ sign and after 1988 when "Accounting regulation for research development" was put in operation the sign was positive $(+)$. All was significant at 1% level. When divided by industry, image, communication and chemistry had a positive $(+)$ affect and wood, rubber and construction metal had a negative $(-)$ effect.[60]

Jae Kyung Lee(2001) insists that Korean KOSDAQ enterprises are indiscriminated. The biggest reason is that traditional companies don't have it and intrinsic value and future value of internet companies are not appropriately evaluated.

It is judged that due to the absence of this evaluation model, internet companies are not evaluated well. Before developing a model for evaluating

---

60) Myung Jang Baek, *Influence of company's research development expense on profit and stock price*, Yonsei University, 1994, pp.93 – 96.

internet companies, she arranged the concept of e−business and compared e−business with traditional companies to find the intrinsic value of e−business. 84 traditional companies were selected from non−high tech industries among KOSPI and KOSDAQ. Regression analysis of book value and net income index showed that traditional companies had 92% explaining ability but the 84 e−businesses only had 71% explaining ability. It was judged that there is an intrinsic value that can not be explained by basic financial statement indexes such as book value and net income.

Regarding the 21% point of company value that can not be explained by traditional company evaluating model as intrinsic value of e−business and the intrinsic value being statistic of web traffic volume, regression analysis was performed using technical statistic and demonstrated variable from correlation analysis. Even though web traffic volume is receiving cold reception as it is not accompanied by sales and profit, it is still the factor for determining the company value of e−business. Also, among 58 e−business companies listed in KOSDAQ, it was analyzed that companies with web traffic volume had higher market value. Firstly, without a time series data. it is somewhat unreasonable to make a conclusion just by using data for a single point in the year 2000. Secondly, web traffic volume was obtained from only 45 companies among total 84 companies and this was used as the determinant for company value of e−businesses. Thirdly, real option concept which is useful for limitless research and measuring company value of e−business was though as a value evaluation model study feasible of generalization. Fourthly, comparison of pure e−business company and e−business with offline was not progressed.[61]

Sae kyung Oh(2000) introduced a value evaluation method to suggest value evaluation model and evaluation method that is effective and ad-

---

61) Jae Kyung Lee(2001), *op. cit.* pp.75−78.

equate for domestic situation of venture companies, by detailed comparative analysis of value evaluation methods for domestic venture companies. She emphasized that the most important difference between value evaluation of listed and unlisted enterprises is the evaluation of investment and business related risk. Risk should be classified as ownership risk and business risk and method of value evaluation should be divided as early stage and after funding to confirm the stage of value. Venture companies show negative (−) cash flow during early stage but after a period of time, they mostly form a cash flow that brings great profit. Therefore American venture capital enterprises use positive cash flow or cash flow of the point when profit is produced to evaluate the value of venture companies. The most important aspect of venture company evaluation is finding a comparative company. After selecting the company for comparison, sales amount multiplier venture capital evaluation method should be used. Then process should be determined considering the funding stage of evaluation subjected venture company.

Analysis result using newly registered companies showed that a comparative company with similar sales amount should be selected when using sales amount multiplier method. When calculating stock price for venture companies that produce profit, multiplying profit per stock and PER is accurate than using sales amount multiplier method.

Other factors that needs to be considered for value evaluation of venture companies are; during bull market, value of unlisted stocks elevate due to the increase of listed or registered stock price and during bear market value of unlisted stocks decline. Therefore, market situation should be considered for venture companies and value evaluation of unlisted stocks.[62]

Jae ok Kim(2002) divided 99 venture companies listed on KOSDAQ into

---

62) Sae Kyung Oh, 『Report on venture enterprise and value evaluation method』, Konkuk University, 2000.

3 groups according to growth and evaluated each group by DCF and real option value. The value of real option value model compared to DCF model was found to be high. It was 151%, 113% and 117% in order of groups with high growth. This result proved that most of the value of venture companies are drafted from growth possibility and option premium, the motive power of growth, is higher in traditional companies compared to venture companies.

Also, company value of real option value model was proved to be very similar to market stock price compared to DCF model. This shows that real option value model is more reasonable for company value evaluation of venture companies.[63]

Jung yoo Kim(2000) presumed the company value of Amazon.com using traditional DCF model and newly spot-lighted real option value model. Value by DCF model was 35.4 billion dollar and real option value model was 26.4 dollar. This was both higher than the market value which was 15.2 billion dollar at that time. She insisted that one can not be judged to be superior than the other and two value evaluation models are not distinct but has very close relationship to each other.

In other words, accurate DCF analysis should be preceded for accurate measurement of real option value regarding value evaluation subjected company. The biggest problem of DCF analysis, uncertainty of prediction, can not be completely eliminated in real option value model as well.

Additionally, usefulness of real option value is the qualitative analysis frame for understanding the various possibility of especially the investment strategy among company's business strategy than a qualitative value of the company.[64]

---

63) Jae Ok Kim(2002), *op. cit.* pp.118-121.

64) Jung Yoo Kim, *Value evaluation of Dot.com through real option, Focusing on company value evaluation cases of Amazon.com, e-biz group,* Working Paper, 2000. 2.

Jae min Park(2001) observed the study of Schwartz&Moon and insisted that methods for transection data of various companies rather than a certain company should be considered. Especially, when evaluating internet companies, it is favorable to proceed conventional value evaluation using DCF with aggressive value evaluation using real option value model. He indicated the reason for unactive positive study based on option theory in Korea.

First: On the contrary of the necessity of various data and evaluation data to apply in option model, market price data is not sufficiently measured yet.

Second: Business formation is unclear such as in cases when necessary company accounting data is not provided and company's business status is differently expressed.[65]

Yoon ho Lee(2007) selected 12 companies for analysis sample among companies listed in KOSDAQ and KOSPI to present an evaluation model and method that can reasonably evaluate food service companies. For the market stock price of each company, highest, lowest and average stock price from January 2004 to December 2006 was drawn out. Using inspection report of 3 years, the research used growth option model from real option models to evaluate the value of food service companies. 5 variables of current price, event price, variableness, event period and riskless rate were used to calculate option value of food service companies and residual value was discount calculated by DCF method then company value was analyzed by the added sum.

Various parameters were drawn out mainly from the data of domestic food service companies and industries. These are applied in the model for positive evaluation of company value.

---

65) Jae Min Park, (STEPI researcher) Resonable company value evaluation of dot.com, Referred to case report, 2001, p.87.

Value of food service company by ROV model was analyzed highly when above the minimum stock price. A group 100%, B group 80% and C group 100%. This showed that most of the value for food service companies were highly judged by option premium which is the motive power of growth. Value of food service companies by DCF model was A group 50%, B group 80% and C group 100% when above the minimum stock price. All of the companies are mixed together. A and B group has high and low companies mixed together which suggests that growth premium possibility has not yet been recognized.[66]

3) Preceding studies of domestic hotel companies

Hyun Joo Ahn(2000) analyzed 5 star hotels and suggested that lowering capital cost by maximized cash flow and increasing sales amount will allow EVA conversion from $(-)$ to $(+)$.[67] Yong sang Ryu(2000) insisted that EVA will increase by lowering capital cost of hotels for natives and increase rooms for chain hotels.[68] Eun A Cho(2001) suggested substantialized management policy by considering capital cost for maximized business value.[69] Chang dae Park(2001) insisted that EVA can be elevated by considering capital cost and disposing capitals that are not related to marketing activity.[70] So yoon Cho and Hyun sook Cho(1998) applied economical value $-$ added and based on inspection report of each hotel, calculated

---

66) Yoon Ho Lee(2007), *op. cit.* p.78.

67) Hyun Joo Ahn, *Study on EVA — Focusing on domestic 5 star hotels,* Sejong University, 2000, pp.55 – 56.

68) Yong Sang Ryu, *Study on profitability of hotel industries — Focusing on 5 star chain hotels and native hotels,* Incheon University, 2000, pp.83 – 84.

69) Eun A Cho, *Study on hotel enterprise value evaluation using EVA — Focusing on 5 star hotels within Seoul,* Sejong University, 2001, pp.83 – 86.

70) Chang Dae Park, *Study on management outcome index of hotels — Focusing on EVA,* Sejong University, 2001, pp.59 – 62.

effective corporate income tax rate and borrowed capital cost to calculate invested capital and NOPLAT.[71] indicated that as domestic hotel industries emphasized external growth policy, management outcome should be conversed to value management with importance on producing pure cash flow and that active introduction of EVA is necessary.

71) So Yoon Cho, Hyun Sook Cho, Study on EVA, 『Korean Academic Society of Hospitality Administration』, 1998, pp.79 – 88.

Chapter 03 Study design and model

1. Data collection and analysis method
2. Study design
3. Research Models

Valuation of hotel – Food & Beverage department –

Study design and model

1 Data collection and analysis method

1) Data collection

Two enterprises in Seoul with 7 years of F&B service in hotel companies were selected. Balance sheet, income statement and cash flow was collected and calculated. From the inspection report by Financial Supervisory Service, balance sheet and income statement during 7 years of the two enterprises were created and parameter value was calculated. Average growth rate was grasped by GDP company growth rate of The Bank of Korea.

2) Analysis method

(1) Total sample

Samples of analysis subjected hotel companies of this study was selected focusing on analysis data during January 2001 to December 2007, excluding reports without same account on financial and income statement from 2001 to 2007. Suspicious F&B businesses with explosive increase in sales amount and distorted evaluation result on income statement were excluded and 2 hotels were selected as sample data.

(2) Constitution of total sample

Sample constitution of business place in A hotel is formed by F&B department, banquet department, beverage business department and other business department. F&B department is formed of 8 places, banquet department 1 place, beverage business department 3 places and other business department 2 places, making total 14 business places.

Detailed business places of F&B department is Korean restaurant (1), Chinese restaurant (1), Japanese restaurant (1), western restaurant (4) and buffet restaurant (1).

Beverage business department is formed with lounge (1), main bar (1), pub style bar (1), Banquet department (1), other business department is formed with room service and deli shop.

B hotel is formed by F&B department, banquet department, beverage business department and other business department. It has food departments (2), beverage departments (2), banquet department (1) other business departments (2), making total 7 business places.

<Table 3-1> shows that food department is operated as buffet and Chinese restaurants. Beverage department is operated as lounge and pub style bar. Banquet department has 1 business place and other business department is operated as room service and deli shop.

〈Table 3-1〉 Statistic comparison of sample hotel business places(A. B hotel)

Classification	A Hotel	B Hotel	A Hotel(%)	B Hotel(%)
Food Department	8	2	57.1	28.6
Beverage Department	3	2	21.5	28.6
Banquet Department	1	1	7.1	14.2
Other Department	2	2	14.3	28.6
Total	14	7	100	100

2 Study design

1) Study method

This study investigated how the result changes when account is applied in the form of DCF model when it is actually applied in a hotel company. Also, this study verifies whether accurate future marketing strategy can be progressed and the differences between each hotel. For accurate value evaluation using DCF model, Terminal Value and NPV(Net present value) was applied which was calculated by Microsoft Office Excel 2007 Program.

Therefore, new technique was introduced through this study and by applying it to hotel related companies, more accurate current and future value evaluation of hotel companies were calculated. Each company needs a substantial management such as sales management cost inventory asset and management of asset cost rather than growth centered policy. Also, in the situation of deepening competition between hotels, accurate company value of the past is necessary for continuos growth and development. Future company strategy should be established based on this.

Two approaching methods were used to achieve the goal of this study and theoretical and positive study method was used together. For image analysis, examination and analysis of theoretical and preceding study was progressed and arranged theoretically.

2) Subject of study

Subjects of this study were selected by the following detailed conditions.

First: Among 14 hotel F&B business places of 14 hotels in Seoul region, income statement, hotel balance sheet and cash flow chart was collected for 5 hotel F&B business places. 2 hotels with high validity and reliability for this study were selected and 21 F&B business places were set as subjects for investigation.

Second: Data analysis period was limited to business places that have been operated form 2001 to 2007.

Third: Company with currently operating F&B business places(F&B department, banquet department, beverage business department and other business department)

3   Research Models

1) Business Valuation Models using Discounted Cash Flow Models[72]

The adjusted discounted cash flow model is a modification of the discounted cash flow model and is used in practical business. The adjusted

---

72) Tom Copeland, tim Koller, and Jack Muurrin, Dong Won Park, Kwang Jun Kim, Soon Poong Park, *Business Valuation*, Kyung Moon Sa,(2005), *op. cit,* pp.109 – 129.

discounted cash flow model adjusts the basic discounted cash flow model, estimates the firm's cash flow during the estimated period and evaluates the remaining period of the firm as the firm's value and all these factors are added up to become the firm's value. The adjusted discounted cash flow model considers continuous re-investment for the firm's growth when it evaluates the cash flow and therefore, the value of the firm's remaining period is recognized as it's value. This method is generally used in traditional business valuation models. The annual discounted cash flow model can be drawn as follows.

$$CF_t = EBIT_t \times (1-T) + DEPR_t - CAPEX - NWC + Other_t$$

$CF = Cash\ Flow.$

$T = Corporation\ Tax\ Rate.$

$DEPR = Depreciation\ Expense.$

$CAPEX = Capital\ Outlay.$

$Other = Accrued\ Expenses\ etc.$

$NWC = Change\ of\ Net\ Working\ Capital.$

With the assumption that after the estimated period, the firm will enter the steady stage and will grow g% each year, the term-end value can be drawn from the perpetuity cash flow formula and is as follows.

$$TV = [\ CF \times (\ 1+g\ )]\ /\ (\ r-g\ )$$

$TV = Term\text{-}end\ Value.$

$r = Rate\ of\ Discount.\ g = Growth\ Rate.$

Therefore, the firm's value in the current period is the sum total of the annual cash flow of the estimated period discounted by the current value and the current value of remaining period value. The formula is as follows .[73]

$$V=\sum_{t=1}^{n}\frac{CF}{(1+r)^t}+\frac{TV}{(1+r)^n}$$

In this case, the cash flow was approached from assets and therefore, the weighted average cost of capital, WACC, was considered for the discount rate. The most essential factor for calculating the WACC is that the definition and consistency must be maintained for the general valuation method and the discounted cash flow that will be discounted.

Therefore, in this case, in order to calculate the WACC, each percentage of the capital structure is multiplied with its earning rate and then added up and also, corporation tax should be excluded from the liabilities before they are added to the sum. Therefore, the discount rate for a firm which raised its capital through common stock and liabilities is as follows.[74]

$$r=\frac{E}{V}r_e+(1-T)\frac{D}{V}r_d$$

$r_e =$ *Stockholders' required rate of return.*

$r_d =$ *Creditors' required rate of return.*

$T =$ *Corporation Tax rate.*

$\dfrac{E}{V} =$ *weight of stocks compared to total firm value.*

$\dfrac{D}{V} =$ *weight of debt compared to total firm value.*

---

73) Jae Kyung Lee(2001), *et passim.*
74) Dong Hwan Kim, Jae Ki Lee(2000), *et passim.*

The required rate of return of investors holding stocks used to raise debt is not the required rate of return of the total stockholders. Therefore, the stockholders' required rate of return is needed. This can be calculated with the Capital Asset Pricing Model(CAPM).

$$r_e = r + \times (RM - r)$$

r_f = Risk free rate(National Bond Return Rate).

RM = rate of earning in market, = Beta of the security.[75]

In addition, although the cash flow model tends to rely on uncertain market forecasts, it can be applied regardless of conditions and also, it can function in situations in which the firm is not listed or there are no samples to compare with. Therefore, the model is definitely a splendid method to evaluate company values. Also, reasonable estimation of future cash flow and discount rate will enable better and accurate evaluations.[76]

2) Business valuation model using the Hamada Model[77]

In order to calculate the WACC, the stock beta must be adjusted to match the use of debts and for indebted firms, the financial risk increases with the increase of leverage and as a result, the stock beta increases. The Hamada Model shows that the stock beta of indebted firms(β_L) can be drawn from the stock beta of non indebted firms(β_v). The Hamada Models

---

75) Value that expresses the sensibility of profit from securities and portfolio towards overall movement of securities market. For example, when stock price increases by 5% during 10% increase of market(general index), value of β is 0.5. In other words, when β is 1, it is completely moving with the market.

76) Bradford Comell(1993), *et passim*.

77) Moon Sung Kim(2003), *op. cit.* pp.12 − 13.

conducts the calculation with the following formula.

$$\beta_L = \beta_U \left[1 + (1-t)\frac{B}{S} \right]$$

The formula was created from MM(1963) adjusted proposition no.1 and the debt beta β_d is set as 0. Therefore, the Hamada Model is based on the following assumptions.

The debt used by firms is risk free($\beta_d = 0$). Therefore, the firm's capital cost of debts is risk free rate of interest.

This assumption is not included in MM(1963) adjusted proposition. Therefore, the Hamada Model is stricter compared to MM(1963) proposition. If the firm's liability is risk free and the liability interest rate is equal to the risk free rate of interest, the WACCs drawn from the MM adjusted proposition and the Hamada Mode are equal, therefore, the same result for both methods.

Chapter 04 Analysis result and interpretation

1. Result of positive analysis

Valuation of hotel – Food & Beverage department –

Analysis result and interpretation

1 Result of positive analysis

1) Value evaluation of DCF model applied business place

Using DCF model, application of various parameters suitable for Korean context and situation was progressed to calculate company value of DCF for Terminal Value and NPV(Net present value). 5, 10 years presumed comparative table of sample hotel on <Table 4-1> and <Table 4-2> by DCF model shows that most of the values for B hotel was higher than A hotel, because of value of presumed asset to profit was high. On the hand, analysis of A hotel using DCF model, NPV was -28.8 billion for economical company value of 5 years. TV was approximately -18.8 billion and DCF value was 10 billion.

The other hand, NPV of B hotel, however, was about 88 billion and TV was 64.9 billion. DCF value was 23.1 billion won and NPV of 5% growth was 188 billion. When assuming a 5% decline, it would fall to about 62 billion from 88 billion.

Economical company value of 10 years showed that B hotel was evaluated at a great range compared to 5 years evaluation of A hotel. Overall results show that B hotel had superior value evaluation for most of the aspects compared to A hotel(supplement detached).

〈Table 4-1〉 5 years presumed comparative table of hotel value evaluation using DCF(A, B hotel)

(unit: million won)

Hotel	NPV	TV	DCF	NPV (w/no growth)	NPV (w/5% growth)	NPV (w/-5% growth)
A 5years	-28,847	-18,791	-10,055	-28,847	-57,763	-21,308
B 5years	88,080	64,951	23,128	88,080	188,025	62,024

〈Table 4-2〉 10 years presumed comparative table of hotel value evaluation using DCF(A, B hotel)

(unit: million won)

Hotel	NPV	TV	DCF	NPV (w/no growth)	NPV (w/5% growth)	NPV (w/-5% growth)
A 10years	-14,400	-1,638	-12,761	-14,400	-16,922	-13,743
B 10years	391,587	289,588	101,998	391,587	837,190	275,414

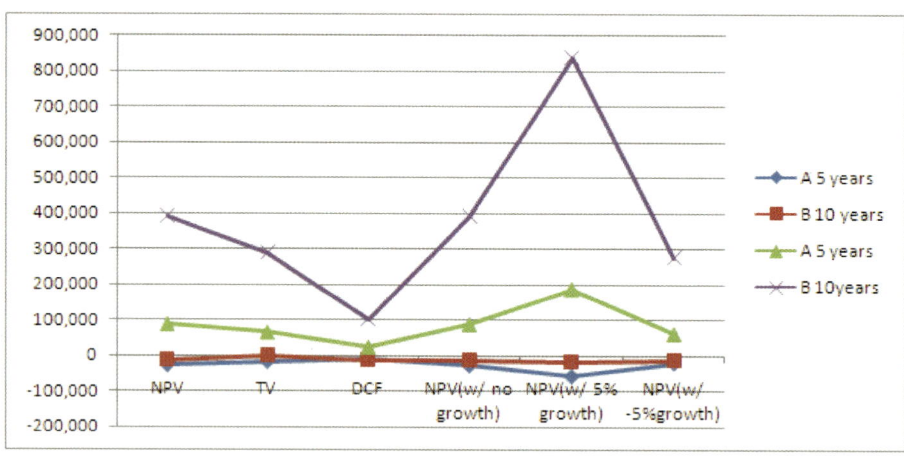

〈Figure 4-1〉 5, 10 years presumed comparative table of hotel value evaluation using DCF(A, B hotel)

5, 10 years presumed comparative table of A hotel value evaluation using DCF on <Table 4 − 3>, <Table 4 − 4> shows that banquet business department has the highest value compared to others. This is because all of the events are progressed by reservation and banquet department had the highest sales amount in A hotel. On the contrary, buffet restaurant had the lowest business place value, due to characteristic of business place has a formation of only producing expenses. Moreover, Lounge bar had the second highest value. This is the representative beverage business place of A hotel as it has a low material cost. Then, room service department comes next highest business place. Value of business place was positive (+) because even though after − tax profit was continuously negative (−), deprecative tangible asset had increased.

The next coming high business place was western restaurant 1(M) and this was because it was operated as membership formation. The reason for negative (−) of 5 years value evaluation by DCF is because of low FCF value. 5 years value of pub style business place was low but in 10 years evaluation, NPV was positive (+) with an about 0.1 billion change from − 0.7 billion and DCF had little change from − 0.39 to − 0.37. Future 10 years progress is looked forward for value of business place.

It also shows that change formation of deli shop was same as pub style business place but all the results had a negative (−) value which expresses low business value.

Business place value of Chinese restaurant was negative (−) as cash outflow is higher than inflow.

Also, all the results for business place evaluation of Japanese restaurant was negative (−). This is because after − tax profit and total cash outflow had continuously decreased. Regarding 10 years economical value evaluation, TV was positive (+) from about − 1.2 billion to 0.1 billion and NPV was also positive (+) from about − 3.1 billion to 0.1 billion. By the overall results, even, it is negative ($-$) for a short term though, it can be expected that after 7 years it would change to positive ($+$).

All the results were negative following the order of Korean restaurant, western restaurant 2 (C), western restaurant 3 (S), western restaurant 4(V), main bar and buffet. This is because after$-$tax profit and cash flow is increasing.

Overall results of A hotel show that economical value of lounge bar, room service, western restaurant 1(M) and banquet business place is high but other departments has low economical value(supplement detached).

〈Table 4$-$3〉 5 years presumed comparative table of business place value evaluation using DCF(A hotel)

(unit: million won)

Hotel	Business Place(sector)	NPV	TV	DCF	NPV(w/no growth)	NPV(w/5% growth)	NPV(w/$-$5% growth))
	Deli Shop	$-$1,235	$-$792	$-$442	$-$1,235	$-$2,454	$-$917
	Lounge Bar	4,550	3,387	1,163	4,450	9,763	3,191
	Room Service	697	528	168	697	1,511	485
	Western Restaurant 1(M)	199	279	$-$79	199	629	87
	Pub Style Bar	$-$749	$-$359	$-$390	$-$749	$-$1,302	$-$605
	Buffet Restaurant	$-$13,365	$-$8,927	$-$4,438	$-$13,365	$-$27,102	$-$9,783
A	Western Restaurant 2 (C)	$-$4,391	$-$2,810	$-$1,581	$-$4,391	$-$8,715	$-$3,264
	Banquet	18,787	11,370	7,417	18,787	36,283	14,226
	Main Bar	$-$6,324	$-$4,775	$-$1,549	$-$6,324	$-$13,673	$-$4,409
	Japanese Restaurant	$-$3,152	$-$1,242	$-$1,909	$-$3,152	$-$5,063	$-$2,653
	Chinese Restaurant	$-$2,001	$-$1,418	$-$583	$-$2,001	$-$4,183	$-$1,432
	Korean Restaurant	$-$4,175	$-$2,619	$-$1,556	$-$4,175	$-$8,205	$-$3,125
	Western Restaurant 3 (S)	$-$5,346	$-$3,340	$-$2,006	$-$5,346	$-$10,486	$-$4,006
	Western Restaurant 4(V)	$-$5,845	$-$3,804	$-$2,041	$-$5,845	$-$11,699	$-$4,319

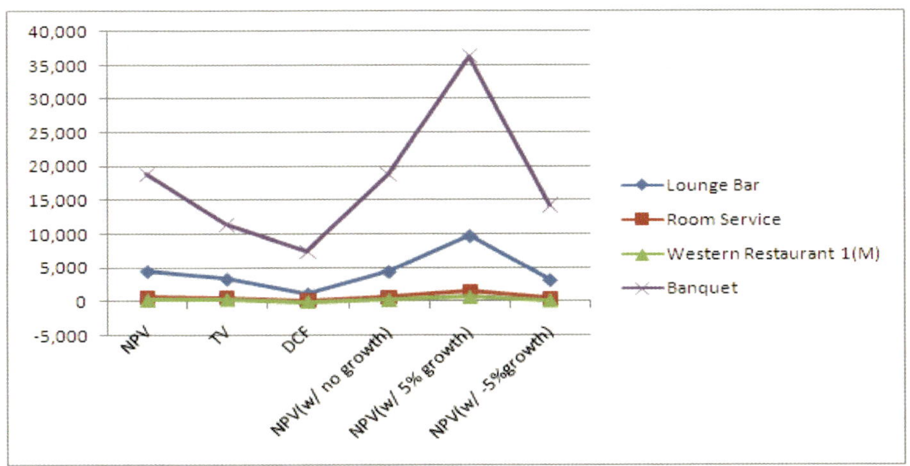

〈Figure 4-2〉 **5 years presumed comparative table of hotel business place (positive+) value evaluation using DCF(A hotel)**

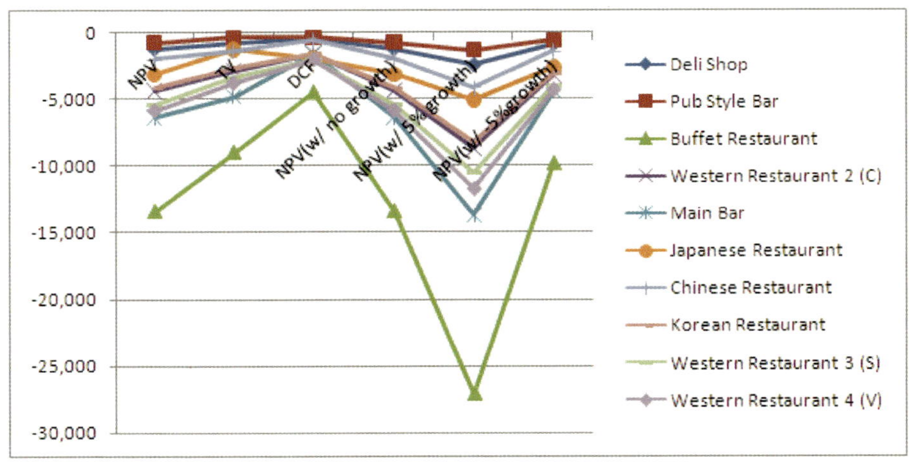

〈Figure 4-3〉 **5 years presumed comparative table of hotel business place (negative -) value evaluation using DCF(A hotel)**

〈Table 4-4〉 **10 years presumed comparative table of business place value evaluation using DCF(A hotel)**

(unit: million won)

Hotel	Business Place(sector)	NPV	TV	DCF	NPV(w/no growth)	NPV(w/5% growth)	NPV(w/-5 % growth))
A	Deli Shop	-876	-254	-622	-876	-1,268	-774
	Lounge Bar	5,555	3,065	2,490	5,555	10,271	4,325
	Room Service	1,417	882	534	1,417	2,774	1,063
	Western Restaurant 1(M)	1,416	1,101	314	1,416	3,111	974
	Pub Style Bar	114	422	-307	114	764	-54
	Buffet Restaurant	-10,961	-4,033	-6,928	-10,961	-17,168	-9,343
	Western Restaurant 2 (C)	-3,436	-1,093	-2,343	-3,436	-5,118	-2,998
	Banquet	25,690	12,322	13,368	25,690	44,651	20,747
	Main Bar	-22,328	-15,887	-6,440	-22,328	-46,775	-15,954
	Japanese Restaurant	-391	1,199	-1,590	-391	1454	-872
	Chinese Restaurant	-932	-133	-798	-932	-1,137	-878
	Korean Restaurant	-2,838	-698	-2,140	-2,838	-3,912	-2,558
	Western Restaurant 3 (S)	-3,841	-1,014	-2,827	-3,841	-5,402	-3,434
	Western Restaurant 4(V)	-4,759	-1,673	-3,086	-4,759	-7,334	-4,088

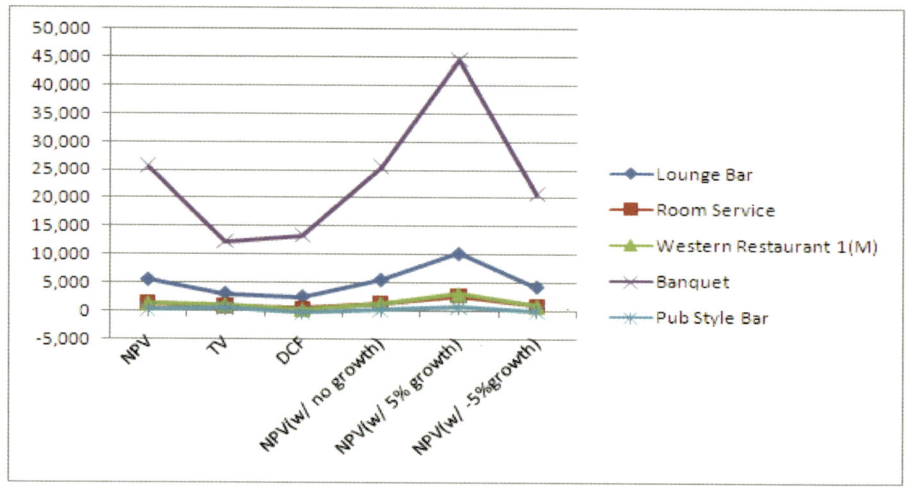

〈Figure 4-4〉 **10 years presumed comparative table of hotel business place (positive+) value evaluation using DCF(A hotel)**

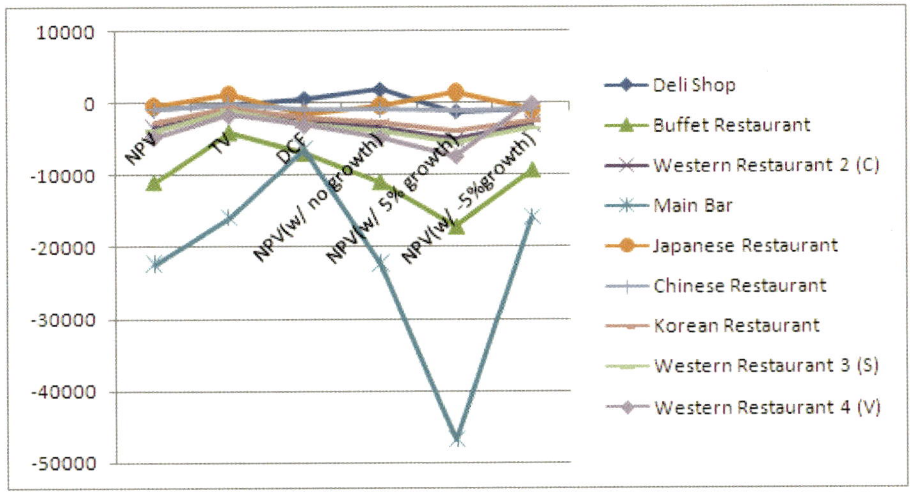

〈Figure 4-5〉 10 years presumed comparative table of hotel business place (negative -) value evaluation using DCF(A hotel)

5, 10 years presumed comparative table of B hotel value evaluation using DCF on <Table 4-5>, <Table 4-6> shows that banquet business department has the highest value compared to others, due to its own characteristic which of all of the events are progressed by reservation and has high after-tax profit and total cash inflow. Banquet department had the highest sales amount in B hotel. On the contrary, deli shop had the lowest business place value. This is because characteristic of business place has a formation of only producing expenses and decrease in after-tax profit and FCF value. Pub style bar had the second highest value. This results on the working capital increases and total cash outflow decreases with operating formation is observed. Buffet hotel is the representative F&B business place of B hotel and has a high sales profit rate. The next following high profit business place was the lounge bar. This is because of bar has low material cost and sales cost rate.

Furthermore, Chinese restaurant had the next highest value. This is because the sales of business place is continuously increasing. The next highest business place was room service due to low material cost.

Overall results of B hotel show that all the business places would be increased and economical value of each business place would elevate(supplement detached).

⟨Table 4-5⟩ 5 years presumed comparative table of business place value evaluation using DCF(B hotel)

(unit: million won)

Hotel	Business Place(sector)	NPV	TV	DCF	NPV(w/no growth)	NPV(w/5% growth)	NPV(w/-5% growth))
B	Deli Shop	-3,098	2,231	-867	-3,098	-6,532	-2,203
	Buffet Restaurant	3,793	2,140	1,653	3,793	7,087	2,934
	Lounge Bar	3,479	2,233	1,245	3,479	6,916	2,583
	Room Service	1,127	750	377	1,127	2,282	826
	Banquet	840,533	710,847	129,685	840,533	1,934,347	555,366
	Chinese Restaurant	2,806	1,856	950	2,806	5,663	2,061
	Pub Style Bar	4,996	4,088	907	4,996	11,287	3,356

⟨Table 4-6⟩ 10 years presumed comparative table of business place value evaluation using DCF(B hotel)

(unit: million won)

Hotel	Business Place (sector)	NPV	TV	DCF	NPV(w/no growth)	NPV(w/5% growth)	NPV(w/-5% growth))
B	Deli Shop	-1,338	-241	-1,097	-1,338	-1,709	-1,241
	Buffet Restaurant	4,585	1,935	2,650	4,585	7,563	3,809
	Lounge Bar	3,974	1,810	2,164	3,974	6,760	3,248
	Room Service	1,358	656	701	1,358	2,367	1,094
	Banquet	480,954	101,135	379,818	480,954	636,577	440,382
	Chinese Restaurant	3,589	1,779	1,810	3,589	6,327	2,875
	Pub Style Bar	6,499	3,825	2,674	6,499	12,385	4,965

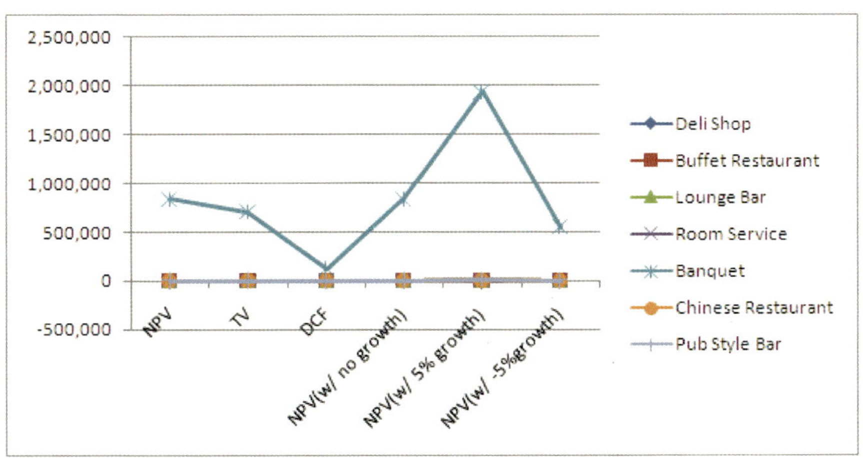

〈Figure 4 − 6〉 5 years presumed comparative table of hotel business place value evaluation using DCF(B hotel)

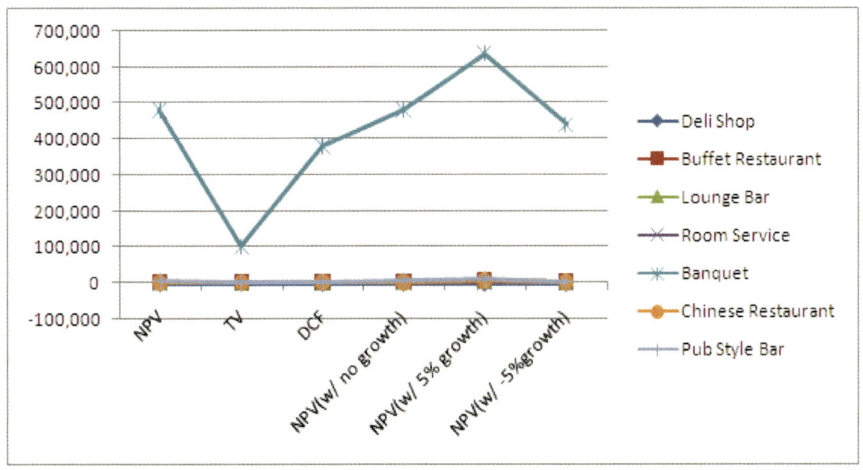

〈Figure 4 − 7〉 10 years presumed comparative table of hotel business place value evaluation using DCF(B hotel)

5, 10 years presumed comparative table of A hotel value evaluation using DCF on <Table 4 − 7>, <Table 4 − 8> regarding business place classification(food, beverage, banquet, others) shows that banquet business place(department) has the highest value compared to others. This is owing to all of the events are progressed by reservation and has the highest NPV.

On the contrary, as result shows that food business place had the lowest business place value. This can be explained by NPV of each business place on <Table 4-3>, <Table 4-4> for 5, 10 years presumed comparative table of A hotel. NPV of western restaurant 1(M) was positive (+) and buffet, western restaurant 2(S) was also negative (-). In addition, NPV of Japanese restaurant, Chinese restaurant, Korean restaurant, western restaurant 3(C) and western restaurant 4(V) were all negative (-). This is because of that total cash outflow is higher than inflow. The second lowest was beverage department(lobby lounge bar and pub style bar). NPV of lounge bar was positive (+) but pub style bar was negative (-).

Results of 5, 10 years value evaluation of other department(deli shop, room service) showed decrease of NPV form -1.2 billion to -0.2 billion and TV is conversed from -0.7 billion to 0.3 billion. Growth rate of introduction stage increased form -2.4 billion to 0.2 billion. This is because of that NPV of room service is positive (+) but deli shop is negative (-). Consequently, overall results of A hotel proved economical value of banquet business place and even though other departments will continuously be negative (-), it may change to positive (+) through long-term improvement of marketing environment. Therefore, beverage and food business place has low economical value as they need great improvement of marketing is required(supplement detached).

⟨Table 4-7⟩ 5 years presumed comparative table of classified business place value evaluation using DCF(A hotel)

(unit: million won)

Hotel	Classification	NPV	TV	DCF	NPV(w/no growth)	NPV(w/5% growth)	NPV(w/-5% growth)
A	Food	-50,868	-32,304	-18,564	-50,868	-100,577	-37,909
	Beverage	-19,626	-13,113	-6,513	-19,626	-39,804	-14,365
	Banquet	18,787	11,370	7,417	18,787	36,283	14,226
	Other	-1,284	-746	-538	-1,284	-2,432	-985

〈Table 4-8〉 10 years presumed comparative table of classified business place value evaluation using DCF(A hotel)

(unit: million won)

Hotel	Classification	NPV	TV	DCF	NPV(w/no growth)	NPV(w/5% growth)	NPV(w/-5% growth))
A	Food	-38,907	-12,057	-26,850	-38,907	-57,461	-34,070
	Beverage	-20,476	-8,996	-11,479	-20,476	-34,320	-16,867
	Banquet	25,690	12,322	13,368	25,690	44,651	20,747
	Other	-220	307	-528	-220	251	-344

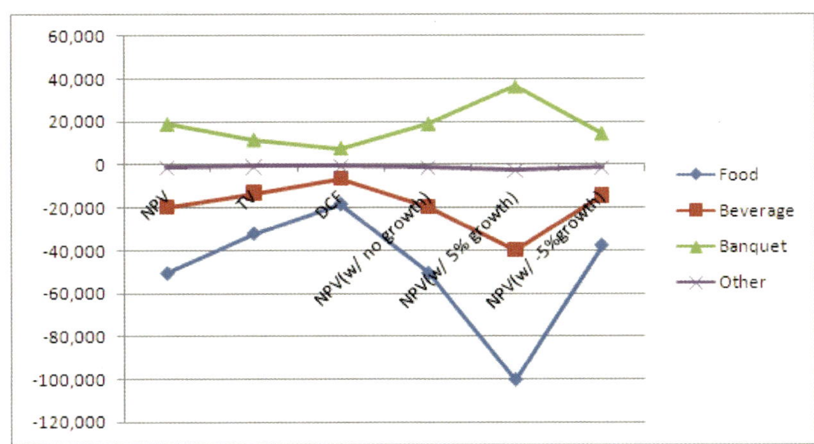

〈Figure 4-8〉 5 years presumed comparative table of hotel business place value evaluation using DCF(A hotel)

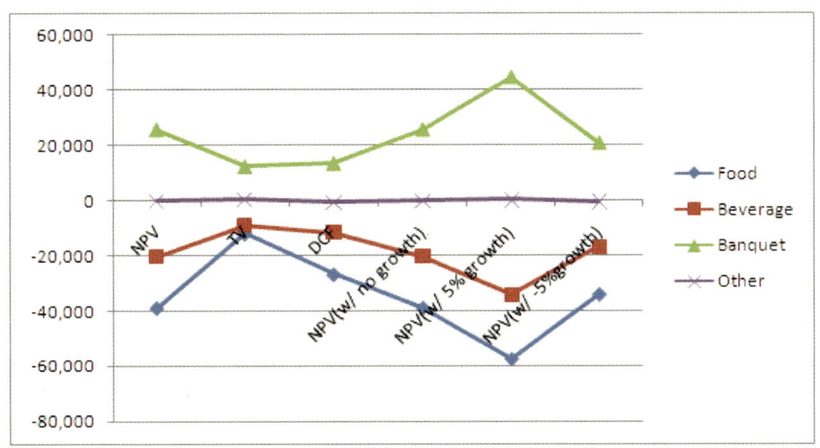

〈Figure 4-9〉 10 years presumed comparative table of hotel business place value evaluation using DCF(A hotel)

5, 10 years presumed comparative table of B hotel value evaluation using DCF on <Table 4-9>, <Table 4-10> regarding business place classification(food, beverage, banquet, others) shows that banquet business place has the highest value compared to others. This is because all of the events are progressed by reservation and has the highest NPV.

On the contrary, food business place had the lowest business place value. This is because characteristic of entire food business place(Chinese restaurant, buffet restaurant) has a formation of only producing expenses. Value evaluation as single business place was positive (+) but NPV showed that cash outflow was higher than cash inflow. Other departments(deli shop, room service) showed same results as food business place.

Overall results of B hotel proved the future value of banquet and beverage business places and showed that food and other business places would continuously show negative (−) with declining economical future value(supplement detached).

〈Table 4-9〉 5 years presumed comparative table of classified business place value evaluation using DCF(B hotel)

(unit: million won)

Hotel	Classification	NPV	TV	DCF	NPV(w/no growth)	NPV(w/5% growth)	NPV(w/−5% growth)
B	Food	−3,133	−2,336	−797	−3,133	−6,729	−2,196
	Beverage	11,817	7,774	4,043	11,817	23,780	8,699
	Banquet	840,533	710,847	129,685	840,533	1,934,347	555,366
	Other	−86	−267	181	−86	−497	21

〈Table 4-10〉 10 years presumed comparative table of classified business place value evaluation using DCF(B hotel)

(unit: million won)

Hotel	Classification	NPV	TV	DCF	NPV(w/no growth)	NPV(w/5% growth)	NPV(w/−5% growth)
B	Food	−1,989	−682	−1,306	−1,989	−3,040	−1,715
	Beverage	17,053	9,136	7,917	17,053	31,112	13,388
	Banquet	480,954	101,135	379,818	480,954	636,577	440,382
	Other	1,908	1,197	711	1,908	3,751	1,428

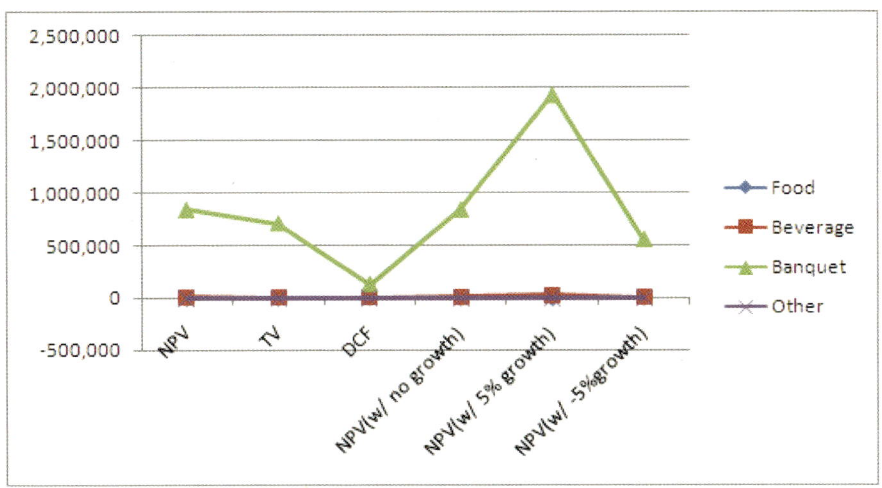

〈Figure 4-10〉 5 years presumed comparative table of hotel business place value evaluation using DCF(B hotel)

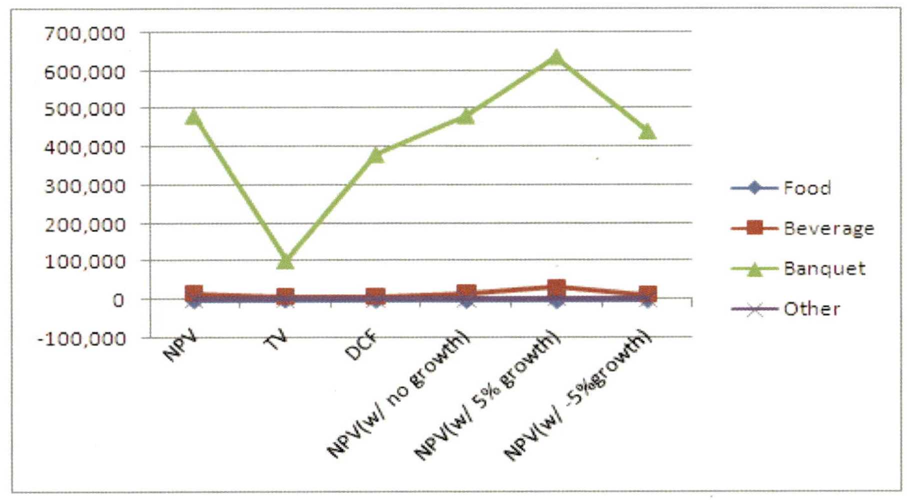

〈Figure 4-11〉 10 years presumed comparative table of hotel business place value evaluation using DCF(B hotel)

5, 10 years presumed comparative table of A hotel classified business place operating formation value evaluation using DCF on <Table 4-11>, <Table 4-12> shows that business place value of eastern restaurant (Japanese, Korean, Chinese) is western restaurant(western 1(M), western

2(S), western 3(C), western 4(V)) business place. Comparison of PV between western and eastern business places, eastern business places show lower values. However, all of the business places are negative $(-)$ as all of the individual are negative $(-)$ and eastern and western business places should go through a big change. Overall results of A hotel show that economical value of eastern and western business places is declining(supplement detached).

〈Table 4-11〉 5 years presumed comparative table of classified business place operating formation value evaluation using DCF(A hotel)

(unit: million won)

Hotel	Classification	NPV	TV	DCF	NPV(w/no growth)	NPV(w/5% growth)	NPV(w/-5% growth)
A	Asian Restaurant	-13,906	-8,223	-5,682	-13,906	-26,561	-10,607
	Western Restaurant	-41,196	-26,604	-14,592	-41,196	-82,133	-30,523

〈Table 4-12〉 10 years presumed comparative table of classified business place operating formation value evaluation using DCF(A hotel)

(unit: million won)

Hotel	Classification	NPV	TV	] DCF	NPV(w/no growth)	NPV(w/5% growth)	NPV(w/-5% growth)
A	Asian Restaurant	-8,755	-1,535	-7,219	-8,755	-11,118	-8,139
	Western Restaurant	-34,050	-11,867	-22,183	-34,050	-52,310	-29,289

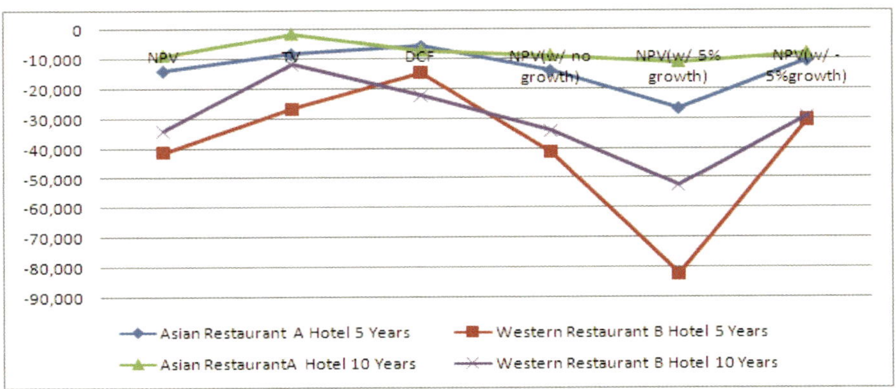

〈Figure 4−12〉 5, 10 years presumed comparative table of hotel business place value evaluation using DCF(A hotel)

5, 10 years presumed comparative table of A, B hotel identical operating business place value evaluation using DCF on <Table 4−13>, <Table 4−14> shows that room service had economical value for both hotels. The reason for different value is because of that the size of business places are different from each other. Therefore, room service business places of A and B hotels are judged to have economical value. Chinese restaurant business place of A hotel had lower economical value compared to B hotel. From this result, Manager of A hotel should find the point for resolute change.

Economical value of buffet restaurant was higher of B hotel compared to A hotel but as most of buffet restaurant has a high reservation rate, A hotel should increase the sales amount and lower the sales cost. Banquet business place had high economical value for both A and B hotels. However, due to the great variation of after−tax profit and cash inflow, it shows that the B hotel had a high result value and it is to be higher than cash outflow. Lounge bar did not show much difference between A and B hotel.

Economical value of pub style bar was higher in B hotel than A hotel(supplement detached).

〈Table 4-13〉 5 years presumed comparative table of sample hotel identical operating business place value evaluation using DCF(A, B hotel)

(unit: million won)

Hotel	Business Place(sector)	NPV	TV	DCF	NPV(w/no growth)	NPV(w/5% growth)	NPV(w/-5% growth)
A	Room	697	528	168	697	1,511	485
B	Service	1,127	750	377	1,127	2,282	826
A	Chinese	-2,001	-1,418	-583	-2,001	-4,183	-1,432
B	Restaurant	2,806	1,856	950	2,806	5,663	2,061
A	Buffet	-13,365	-8,927	-4,438	-13,365	-27,102	-9,783
B	Restaurant	3,793	2,140	1,653	3,793	7,087	2,934
A	Banquet	18,787	11,370	7,417	18,787	36,283	14,226
B		840,533	710,847	129,685	840,533	1,934,347	555,366
A	Lounge Bar	4,550	3,387	1,163	4,450	9,763	3,191
B		3,479	2,233	1,245	3,479	6,916	2,583
A	Pub Style Bar	-749	-359	-390	-749	-1,302	-605
B		4,996	4,088	907	4,996	11,287	3,356

〈Table 4-14〉 10 years presumed comparative table of sample hotel identical operating business place value evaluation using DCF(A, B hotel)

(unit: million won)

Hotel	Business Place(sector)	NPV	TV	DCF	NPV(w/no growth)	NPV(w/5% growth)	NPV(w/-5% growth)
A	Room	1,417	882	534	1,417	2,774	1,063
B	Service	1,358	656	701	1,358	2,367	1,094
A	Chinese	-932	-133	-798	-932	-1,137	-878
B	Restaurant	3,589	1,779	1,810	3,589	6,327	2,875
A	Buffet	-10,961	-4,033	-6,928	-10,961	-17,168	-9,343
B	Restaurant	4,585	1,935	2,650	4,585	7,563	3,809
A	Banquet	25,690	12,322	13,368	25,690	44,651	20,747
B		480,954	101,135	379,818	480,954	636,577	440,382
A	Lounge Bar	5,555	3,065	2,490	5,555	10,271	4,325
B		3,974	1,810	2,164	3,974	6,760	3,248
A	Pub Style Bar	114	422	-307	114	764	-54
B		6,499	3,825	2,674	6,499	12,385	4,965

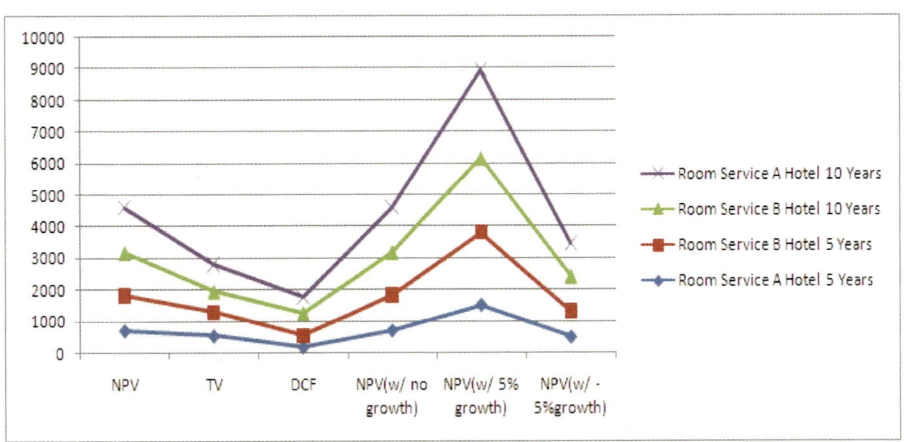

〈Figure 4-13〉 5, 10 years presumed comparative table of sample hotel identical operating business place value evaluation using DCF(A, B hotel)

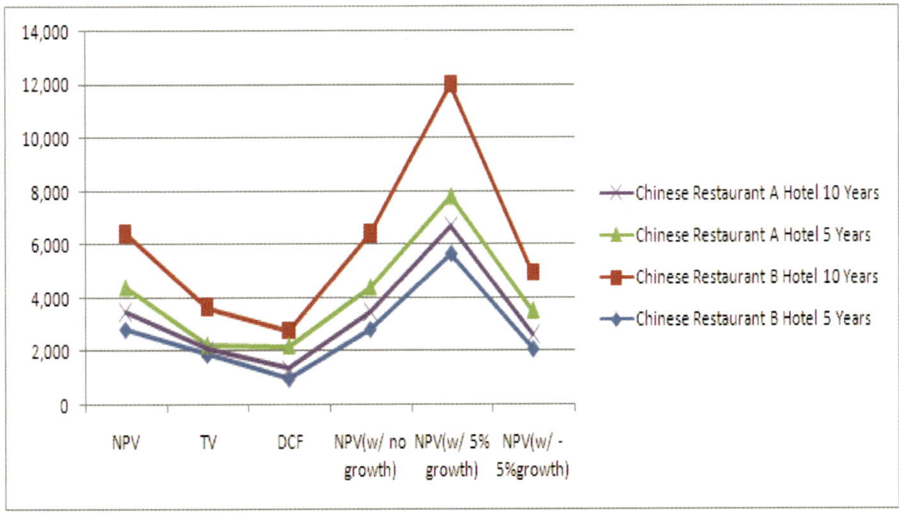

〈Figure 4-14〉 5, 10 years presumed comparative table of sample hotel identical operating business place value evaluation using DCF(A, B hotel)

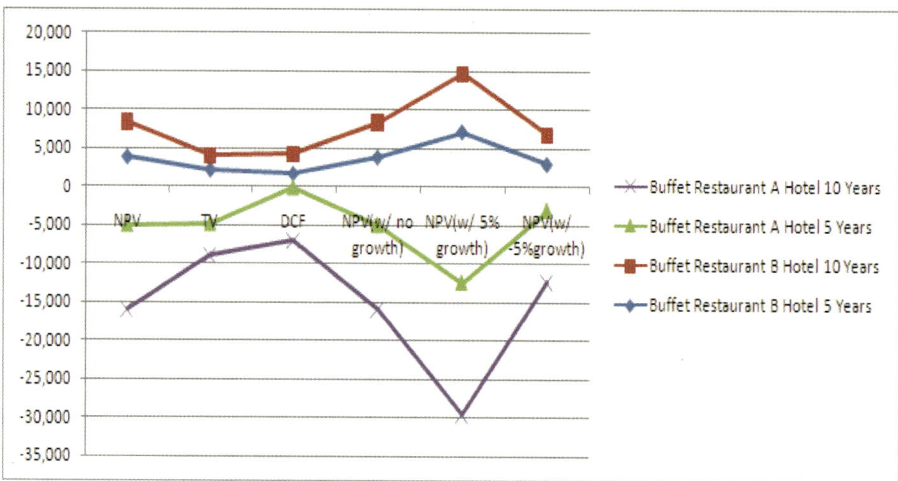

〈Figure 4-15〉 5, 10 years presumed comparative table of sample hotel identical operating business place value evaluation using DCF(A, B hotel)

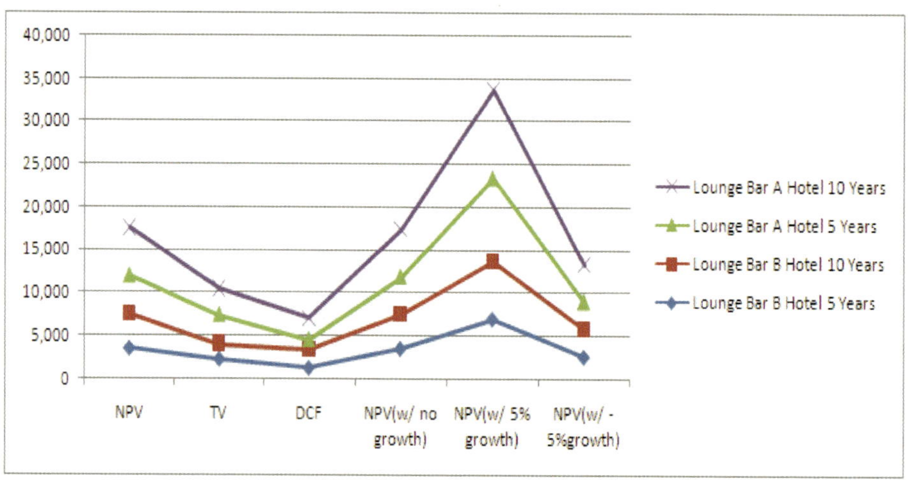

〈Figure 4-16〉 5, 10 years presumed comparative table of sample hotel identical operating business place value evaluation using DCF(A, B hotel)

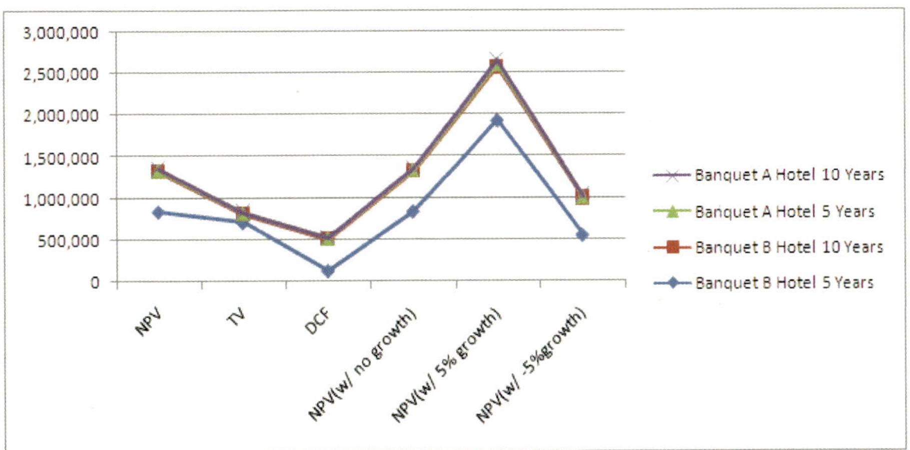

〈Figure 4-17〉 5, 10 years presumed comparative table of sample hotel identical operating business place value evaluation using DCF(A, B hotel)

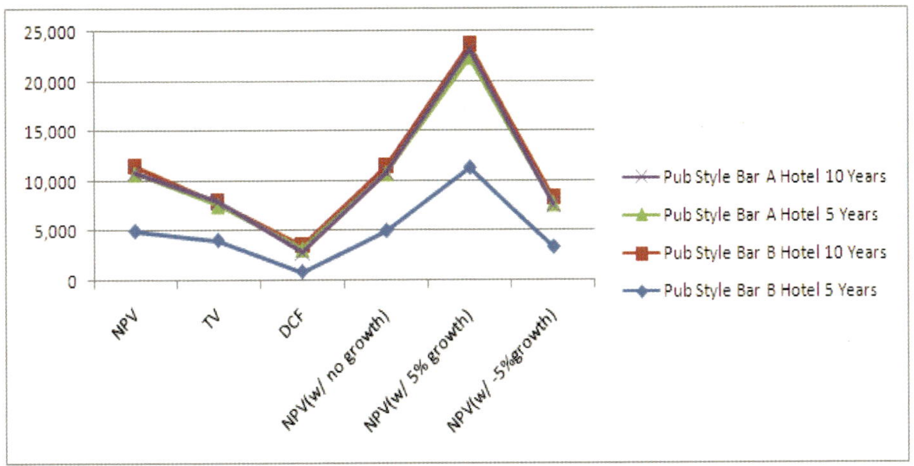

〈Figure 4-18〉 5, 10 years presumed comparative table of sample hotel identical operating business place value evaluation using DCF(A, B hotel)

2) Income statement comparison of sample hotels' business places

The below <Table 4-15> shows the income structures of hotel A's business places. The ratio of total sales to profit is an index for valuating profitability and is come up by dividing net operating income by amount of sales. The results show that the lounge bar has the highest profit ratio of 9.8%. The business place with the lowest profit ratio was the western restaurant 1(M), -47.3%, followed by -39.2% of the western restaurant 2(S), main bar -28.1%, Korean restaurant -24.8%, Japanese restaurant -23.8%, western restaurant 3(C) -18.3%, room service -17.1%, western restaurant 4(V) -15.8%, pub style bar -14.2%, buffet restaurant -5%, deli shop -3.2%, Chinese restaurant -2.3% and the banquet hall, -0.2%. In total, the minus (-) results indicate that there are no business values for the food and beverage business.

The cost of sales is required for earning operation revenues and is counted by cost of sales/amount of sales. Lower results indicate higher rate of returns. Also, the account details of hotel A's cost of sales are material costs, personal expenses and direct expenses. The lounge bar showed the lowest result of 68.2% and the room service was the highest with 120%. Other results were 104.9% for western restaurant 1(M) and 104.3% for western restaurant 2(S). The Korean restaurant was 96.3% and the western restaurant 3(C) 94.3%, western restaurant 4(V) 88.5%, pub style bar 86.6%, deli shop 84.4%, buffet restaurant 83.6%, Chinese restaurant 80.1%, main bar 78.6% and the banquet hall 70.3%. Hotel A's ratio of amount of sales to cost of sales showed an average of 89.5%.

Material cost (food costs, beverage costs, other expenses) is a type of cost that accrues in actual business operation. The lower the material cost is, the higher the value of the business place. The results show that the lounge bar's 12.5% was the lowest value and the highest value was the 32.4% of the buffet restaurant. The deli shop was 30%, western restaurant 4(V) 29.5%, Japanese restaurant 29.3%, Chinese restaurant 28%, western restaurant 1(M) 27.5%, western restaurant 2(S) 27.2%, Korean restaurant 24.8% and the western restaurant 3(C) was 23.6%. The main bar was 20.9%, 20.1% for room service, pub style bar 17.9% and 17.8% for the banquet hall. This result suggests that business places with high material costs should be considered to stop their operations in the future.

Personal expenses are equally distributed to all employees and it should be low for high value businesses. Room service showed the highest result for personal expenses followed by the sequence of western restaurant 1(M), western restaurant 3(C), western restaurant 2(S), Korean restaurant, pub style bar, Japanese restaurant, western restaurant 4(V), buffet restaurant, main bar, deli shop, Chinese restaurant and the banquet hall.

The gross profit net sales ratio shows the relation between gross profit and total sales and is figured out by comparing the gross profit with the total sales of 100%. Therefore, the ratio is the index for valuating the profitability of a business. The gross profit net sales ratio is a general standard and there are no fixed standard ratios. Moreover, it also can differ from the type and size of businesses but higher numbers indicate that the firm's sales, manufacturing or purchase operations were well conducted. In this case, the lounge bar showed the highest results followed by the banquet hall, main bar, Chinese restaurant, deli shop, pub style bar, western restaurant 4(V), Japanese restaurant, western restaurant 3(V) and the Korean restaurant. The western restaurant 2(S) and room service showed minus ($-$) results.

The selling administrative cost for hotel A is divided into a per capita basis and the average of the total was 16.5%.

In total, the lounge bar and banquet hall showed the highest results for income structure and can be evaluated as high value business places and the western restaurant 1(M), western restaurant 2(S), Japanese restaurant and Korean restaurant showed low sales management costs

〈Table 4-15〉 Estimated income structure of sample hotel business places(2008~2017), (A hotel)

(unit: %)

Business Place(sector)	Operating Income / Sales account (Estimated Average)	Cost of Sales / Sales account (Estimated Average)	Material Cost / Sales account (Estimated Average)	Personal Expenses/ Sales account (Estimated Average)	Gross profit / Sales account (Estimated Average)	Selling Administrative / Sales account (Estimated Average)
Deli Shop	-3.2	84.4	30	37.1	15.6	14.2
Lounge Bar	9.8	68.2	12.5	35.7	31.8	16.1
Room Service	-17.7	120.7	20.1	82.9	-20.7	18.7
Western Restaurant 1(M)	-47.3	104.9	27.5	55	-4.9	15.7
Pub Style Bar	-14.2	86.8	17.9	49.6	13.2	17.9
Buffet Restaurant	-5.0	83.6	32.4	39.4	16.4	14.8
Western Restaurant 2(S)	-39.2	104.3	27.2	52.7	-4.3	17.2
Banquet	-0.2	70.3	17.8	30.6	29.7	17.5
Main Bar	-28.1	78.6	20.9	38.1	21.4	17.6
Japanese Restaurant	-23.8	91.1	29.3	45.9	8.9	15.8
Chinese Restaurant	-2.3	80.1	28	35.4	19.9	15.3
Korean Restaurant	-24.8	96.4	24.8	50.4	3.6	17.7
Western Restaurant 3(C)	-18.3	94.3	23.6	52.8	5.7	16.8
Western Restaurant 4(V)	-15.8	88.5	29.5	42.1	11.5	15.8

The <Table 4-16> shows the income structure for hotel B's business places. The profit to net sales ratio is a index for judging profitability and is calculated by net operating income/amount of sales. The results ranked the banquet hall's profit ratio of 38.4% as top and the deli shop's -20.8%

was the lowest. The room service was -9.8%, Chinese restaurant -4.8%, pub style restaurant -3.7% and the buffet restaurant -1.6%. On the other hand, the lounge bar showed plus $(+)$ results of 1.5%. In conclusion, business places with plus $(+)$ results have food and beverage business values.

The cost of sales is required for earning operation revenues and is calculated by cost of sales/amount of sales. Lower result indicates higher rate of returns. Also, the account details of hotel B's cost of sales are material costs, personal expenses and direct expenses. The banquet hall showed the lowest digits of 65% and the room service was the highest with 157.6%. The pub style bar was 102.1%, buffet restaurant 81.6%, deli shop 80.5%, Chinese restaurant 79.6% and the lounge bar 63.5%. As a result, the total ratio of amount of sales to cost of sales for hotel B was 89.9%.

Material cost(food costs, beverage costs, other expenses) is a type of cost that accrues in actual business operation. The lower the material cost is, the higher the value of the business place. The lobby lounge bar showed the lowest result of 13.1% and the buffet restaurant showed the highest result of 33.7%. Others were 17.6% for banquet hall, pub 25.9%, Chinese restaurant 26.8% and deli shop 32.5%. The results indicate that business places with high material costs should be closed in the future.

Personal expenses are equally distributed to all employees and it should be low for high value businesses. The banquet room ranked top as the lowest personal expense business place followed by the lounge bar, buffet restaurant, deli shop and Chinese restaurant showing same results and the room service showing the highest digits.

The gross profit net sales ratio shows the relation between gross profit and total sales and is calculated by comparing the gross profit with the total sales of 100%. Therefore, the ratio is the index for valuating the profitability of a business. The gross profit net sales ratio is a general standard and there are no fixed standard ratios. Moreover, it also can differ from the type and size of businesses but higher numbers indicate that the firm's sales, manufacturing or purchase operations were well conducted. In this case, the results were organized in the sequence of lounge bar as top followed by banquet hall, Chinese restaurant, deli shop and the buffet restaurant. The pub and room service showed minus (−) results.

The selling administrative cost for hotel B is divided into a per capita basis and the average of the total was 11.75%.

In total, the lounge bar and banquet hall showed the highest results for income structure and can be evaluated as high value business places and the room service and deli shop showed low income structures.

〈Table 4 - 16〉 Estimated income structure of sample hotel business places(2008~2017)
(B hotel)

(unit: %)

Business Place(sector)	Operating Income / Sales account (Estimated Average)	Cost of Sales /Sales account (Estimated Average)	Material Cost / Sales account (Estimated Average)	Personal Expenses/ Sales account (Estimated Average)	Total Net Sales/ Sales account (Estimated Average)	Selling Administrative /Sales account (Estimated Average)
Deli Shop	− 20.8	80.5	32.5	36.7	19.5	9.6
Buffet Restaurant	− 1.6	81.6	33.7	34.7	18.4	11
Lounge Bar	1.5	63.5	13.1	29.6	36.5	11.3
Room Service	− 9.8	157.6	21	111.1	− 57.6	13
Banquet	38.4	65	17.6	26.1	35	14.5
Chinese Restaurant	− 4.8	79.6	26.8	36.7	20.4	10.9
Pub Style Bar	− 3.7	102.1	25.9	44.6	− 2.1	11.8

3) DCF of sample hotel and comparison, evaluation of estimated income statements(A, B Hotel)

With close examination of the sample hotels' DCF(Discounted Cash Flow) and the ratio of total sales to profit in the below <Table 4−17>, you can see that the banquet hall has the highest NPV for 5 to 10 years and shows that it has the highest business value, but the rate of profit was −0.2(%), just below the lounge bar.

However, the main bar had the lowest NPV but its profit rate was higher than the western restaurant1(M) and the western restaurant2(S) and the ratio of total sales to profit was −28.1(%).

The buffet restaurant showed the second lowest value. The 5year NPV decreased from approximately −13.3 billion won to −10 billion won. The rate of profit was −5.0(%), a higher value compared to other business places. The western restaurant4(V), 3(C) and 2(S) showed low NPV values but the profit rate was −15.8(%), −18.3(%) and −39.2(%) each, showing that the western restaurant 2(S) has the highest rate of profit.

However, for eastern restaurants, the NPV approximately −2.8 billion won for the Korean restaurant, −0.9 billion won for the Chinese restaurant and −0.3 billion won for the Japanese restaurant. The rate of profit was −24.8(%), −2.3(%) and −23.8(%) each, the Chinese restaurant showing the highest rate of profit.

Also, the deli shop's ratio of total sales to profit was −3.2(%) and the NPV showed a plus (+) value. The rate of profit on sales for the room service, pub style bar and western restaurant1(M) was −17.7(%), −14.2(%) and 9.8(%) each. In result, the lounge bar turned out to be the best business place for the rate of profit on sales.

When valuated with the NPV, the 5 years business places of hotel A were sorted out in the sequence of the banquet hall ranking top and followed by the lounge bar, room service, western restaurant 1(M), pub style bar, deli shop, Chinese restaurant, Japanese restaurant, Korean restaurant, western restaurant 2(S), western restaurant 3(C), western restaurant 4(V), main bar and the buffet restaurant. The result of 10 years value analysis found out much differentiation compared to the 5 years analysis in which the banquet hall ranked at top and the others appearing in the sequence of the lounge bar, room service, western restaurant 1(M), pub style bar, Japanese restaurant, deli shop, Chinese restaurant, Korean restaurant, western restaurant 2(S), western restaurant 3(C), western restaurant 4(V), buffet restaurant and the main bar. However, when the income structure analyzed, the lounge bar ranked top and the banquet hall, Chinese restaurant, deli shop, buffet restaurant, pub style bar, western restaurant 4(V), room service, western restaurant 3(C), Japanese restaurant, Korean restaurant, main bar, western restaurant 2(S) and the western restaurant 1(M) were followed.

〈Table 4-17〉 Comparison of DCF(Discounted Cash Flow) and estimated ratio of amount of sales to return on sales(A hotel)

(unit: million won, %)

Business Place(sector)	NPV(5 year)	NPV(10 year)	Operating Income / Sales account (10 year)
Deli Shop	-1,235	-876	-3.2
Lounge Bar	4,550	5,555	9.8
Room Service	697	1,417	-17.7
Western Restaurant 1(M)	199	1,416	-47.3
Pub Style Bar	-749	114	-14.2
Buffet Restaurant	-13,365	-10,961	-5.0
Western Restaurant 2(S)	-4,391	-3,436	-39.2
Banquet	18,787	25,690	-0.2
Main Bar	-6,324	-22,328	-28.1
Japanese Restaurant	-3,152	-391	-23.8
Chinese Restaurant	-2,001	-932	-2.3
Korean Restaurant	-4,175	-2,838	-24.8
Western Restaurant 3(C)	-5,346	-3,841	-18.3
Western Restaurant 4(V)	-5,845	-4,759	-15.8

With close examination of the below <Table 4-18> showing the DCF(Discounted Cash Flow) and the ratio of total sales to profit of the sample hotel (hotel B 5 years − 10 years), you can see that the banquet hall shows the highest NPV for both 5 years and 10 years. The result indicates that the banquet hall is the highest value business place and the rate of profit was 38.4(%) in average, the highest value in the result.

However, the business place showing the lowest NPV was the deli shop and it was also the business place to show the lowest rate of profit of − 20.8(%), indicating that new management strategies will be needed in the future.

The second lowest business place was the room service. The results showed 5 year value of 1.1 billon won increasing to 1.3 billion won in the 10 year value and the profit rate was − 9.8(%), higher than the deli shop. NPV for the Chinese restaurant, lounge bar, buffet restaurant, pub style bar were approximately 2.8 billion won, 3.4 billion won, 3.7 billion won, 4.9 billion won each.

However, on the contrary to expectation, the rankings for profit rates were different. The results showed room service − 9.8(%), Chinese restaurant − 4.8(%), pub style bar − 3.7(%), buffet restaurant − 1.6(%) and the lounge bar 1.5(%). The results show that the rankings are mixed up between the NPV value and the rate of profit.

The NPV value analysis results ranked the 5 to 10 years business places of hotel B in the sequence of the banquet hall at top followed by the pub style bar, buffet restaurant, lounge bar, Chinese restaurant, room service and the deli shop. The income structure analysis results in ranking the banquet hall at top followed by the lounge bar, buffet restaurant, pub style bar, Chinese restaurant, room service and the deli shop at the bottom.

〈Table 4-18〉 Comparison of DCF(Discounted Cash Flow) and estimated
ratio of amount of sales to return on sales(B hotel)

(unit: million won, %)

Business Place(sector)	NPV(5 year)	NPV(10 years)	Operating Income / Sales account (10 year)
Deli Shop	-3,098	-1,338	-20,8
Buffet Restaurant	3,793	4,585	-1,6
Lounge Bar	3,479	3,974	1,5
Room Service	1,127	1,358	-9,8
Banquet	840,533	480,954	38,4
Chinese Restaurant	2,806	3,589	-4,8
Pub Style Bar	4,996	6,499	-3,7

Chapter 05 Conclusion and Suggestions

Valuation of hotel – Food & Beverage department –

Conclusion and Suggestions

This study was conducted under the purpose to find an accurate business valuation index which can enable the firm to survive in the current hotel market of extreme competition. The study realistically analyzed the valuation index of the current and future value of a food and beverage business by using the DCF Model and its concepts.

However, a reasonable business valuation method is essential for the business strategy of hotel companies. Korea has not yet introduced a logical and reasonable valuation model for valuating hotel businesses.

The study used 2 hotel firms as an analyze sample to introduce a new reasonable valuation model that can evaluate the current value of hotel businesses and from these 2 samples, we extracted data from January, 2001 to December, 2007. These data include financial statements of each firm and the income statement and cash flow statement of each place of business. The 7 years period data was used to create a valuation model for each office. Estimated NOPAT, net working capital, NPV, estimated period and discount rate were used as variables for evaluating the value of each place of business and the discounted cash flow model was used to discount and calculate the remaining value. These 2 values were then added up to accurately draw the total value of each place of business.

The parameter data used in this method were all mainly extracted from Korea's food service industry and applied to the model, enabling realistic evaluation.

The DCF Model used in the study showed the value for each place of business of hotel A and hotel B. Hotel B received better results and was generally valuated to possess a high financial validity for most of its values. In specific, out of 14 business places of hotel A, which are 8 food service, 3 beverage service, 1 banquet hall and 2 others, 4 business places were valuated to have financial validity. For hotel B, 2 food service, 2 beverage service, 1 banquet hall and 2 others, 6 business places had financial validity and 1 had low financial validity, showing that hotel B's future value will be higher than hotel A.

We plan to correctly show the current and future value of hotel businesses and find a reasonable valuation model and method for hotel business places. The main purpose of this plan is for the bright future of the hotel industry. Therefore, the DCF Model, which can appropriately show and valuate the special features of the hotel industry, should be used as the valuation method for hotel business places.

The DCF Model used in the study for business valuation has limits. We suggest further studies based on this study.

First, as a method of the study, accurate data is essential for using the research model to correctly valuate the current and future value of hotel businesses and to plan a future management strategy and these data will enable to question the reasonableness of the valuation results. Therefore, the study will be able to provide information and help to those managers planning to invest in the hotel industry.

Second, future studies should be conducted on the research of creating a

DCF Model that can include non－financial variables in its analyze and also the techniques required for the model.

Therefore, continuous future studies are required to apply the DCF Model method to Korea's hotel industry. Also, as the hotel industry is yet in the phase of growth, in order to increase the reasonableness and accuracy of business valuation, new models and methods based on various businesses, new projects and management strategies should be created. These studies will be able to invent a perfect model for valuating business developments and each place of business.

References

1. Domestic References

Ki Young Kim and 2 others, 『*Foodservice Management*』, Hyun Hak Sa, 2000.

Dong Hwan Kim, Jae Ki Lee, 『*Modern Business Management Analysis*』, Doo Nam Sa, 2000.

Chan Il Kim, 『*Newest Company Valuation*』, Kyung Moon Sa, 2005.

Hyo Suk Kang, Won Heum Lee, Jang Yeon Cho, 『*Business Valuation*』, Hong Moon Sa, 2005.

Eui Kyung Lee, 『*Finance management −Theory and application*』, Kyung Moon sa, 2005.

Han Kyu Jung, Chul Jung Kim, Pyeong Sik Yoon, 『*Valuation*』, Kyung Moon Sa, 2002.

Young Do Kwon, *Influence of company financial characteristic on accounting regulation − Focusing on depreciation method and inventory asset evaluation method*, Kyungbuk University, 1991.

Moon Sung Kim, *Traditional WACC, Miles −Ezzel model and value evaluation of listed enterprises using APV*, Kyung Hee University, 2003.

Moon Chul Kim, Role of accounting data on the issue price of newly subscribed stock 『*Accounting study*』 No.19, 1994.

Moon Hyun Kim, *Influence of company characteristic on company value evaluation using accounting data*, Seoul University, 1998.

Jae Ok Kim, *A Study on Reasonable valuation of Venture Company by ROV*, Ho −Seo Univ. Ph.D Dissertation, 2002.

Jung Yoo Kim, *Value evaluation of Dot.com through real option, Focusing on company value evaluation cases of Amazon.com*, e −biz group, 『Working Paper』, 2. 2000.

Yong Sang Ryu, *Study on profitability of hotel industries — Focusing on 5 star chain hotels and native hotels*, In cheon University. 2000.

Jae Min Park, (STEPI researcher) *Resonable company value evaluation of dot.com*, Referred to case report. 2001.

Chang Dae Park, *Study on management outcome index of hotels — Focusing on EVA*, Sejong University, 2001.

Myung Jang Baek, *Influence of company's research development expense on profit and stock price*, Yonsei University, 1994.

Seung Woo Baek, *Comparative analysis of managing achievements between chain hotel and domestic hotel*, Konkuk University, 2006.

Sung Su Seol, *A Theoretical Framework for the Valuation of Technology*, Korea Technology Innovation Society, 3 − 1, 2000.

Seung Myo Shin, *Valuation of stock price using accounting data*, Seoul University, 1995.

Hyun Joo Ahn, *Study on EV — Focusing on domestic 5 star hotels*, Sejong University, 2001.

Sae Kyung Oh, *Report on venture enterprise and value evaluation method*, Konkuk University. 2000.

In Soon Lee, *Study on selecting motive of accounting regulation within managers*, Youngnam University, 1994.

Yoon Ho Lee, *A Study on Valuation of Food Service related Company, ROV and DCF model of Listed Company*, Kyonggi University, 2008.

Joon Hwan Lee, *Value relationship of intangible asset data*, Kyung Hee University, 2001.

Jae Kyung Lee, *A Study on Deciding Value Factor of Korean E − Business Company*, Kyung Hee Univ. Ph.D Thesis, 2001.

Choon Ryul Yoo, *Study on value relation of variables for company value evaluation according to company characteristic*, Seoul University, 1999.

Chu Ran Jung, *Study on value revaluation of Korean KOSDAQ enterprises − role of non − linear model and non − financial data*, Kyung Hee University, 2003

Hye Young Jung, *Price determining model by accounting value*, 『Accounting study』(20; 1), 1995.

So Yoon Cho, Hyun Sook Cho, *Study on EVA*, 『Korean Academic Society of Hospitality Administration』. 1998.

Eun A Cho, *Study on hotel enterprise value evaluation using EVA − Focusing on 5 star hotels within Seoul*, Sejong University, 2001.

Jung Ho Choi, *Influence of advertisement expense and research development expense on company value: Positive analysis by Tobin Q*, 『Accounting study』, No.19, 1994.

Bong Hee Han, *Positive study on the possibility of usefulness increase for financial profit data in domestic capital market*, 『Accounting study』(No.9), 1998.

Joung Chun Lee and Woong Rack Oh, Study on the difference of relevance in company value evaluation model according to company characteristic: Focusing on KOSDAQ regular companies and venture companies, 『Accounting study』(29; 2), 2004.

Hyun Lee, Sang Ki Chang, *Financial statement analysis and investment strategy according to company's intrinsic value determination*, 『Accounting study』(20; 1), 1995.

2. Foreign References

Amir, E., and B. LEV, *Value − Relevance of intangible Information: The Wireless Communication Industry*, Journal of Accounting & Economics: 1996, pp.3 − 30.

Aswath, *Investment Valuation*; Tools and Techniques for Determining the Value of any Asset, John Wiley&Sons, Inc, pp.219 − 234.

Bernard, V. L. *Accounting −based Valuation Methods, Determinants of Market −to −Book Ratios*, and Implication for Financial Statement Analysis, Working Paper, University of Michigan, 1994, pp.305 − 340.

Bernard, V, The *Feltham −Ohlson Framework: Implications for Empiricists*, Contemporary Accounting Research, Vol.11(2) Spring, 1995, pp.733 − 747.

Biddle, G., P. Chen and G. Zhang, *When Capital Follows Profitability: Non −Linear Residual Income Dynamics*, Review of Accounting Studies(June/September), 2001, pp.229 − 265.

Bradford Comell, 『Corporate Valuation』, IrWin, 1993, pp.83 − 84.

Burgstahler, D., and I. *Dichev, Earning, Adaptation, and Equity Value*, The Accounting Review, (April), 1997, pp.187 − 216.

Collins, D. W., E. Maydew, and I. Weiss, Changes in the Value − Relevance of Earning and Book Values over the Past Forty Year, *Journal of accounting and Economics* Vol.24. Issue 1, 1997, pp.39 − 67.

Easton & Harris, *Empirical Evidence on the Relevance of Earnings and Book Value of*

Owners' Equity in Security Valuation, Working paper, Columbia University, 1991.

E S & M. Schwart, Moon, Rational Pricing of Internet Companies, *Financial Analysts Journal*, No.3, 2000.

G. A. Feltham and J. A. Ohlson, *Valuation and Clean Surplus Accounting for Operations and Financial Activities Contemporary Accounting Research*, Vol.11(Spring), 1995, pp.689 − 731.

Hayn, C., The Information Content of Losses, *Journal of Accounting and Economics-(september)*: 1995, pp.125 − 153.

Hirschey, M. Intangible Capital Aspects of Advertising and R&D Expenditures, *Journal of Industrial Economics*, NO.1, 1982.

Ely & Waymyre, Intangible Assets and Stock Price in the Pre − SEC Era. *Journal of Accounting Research*, 1999, pp.17 − 51.

J, Williams, *The Theory of Investment Value*, Cambridge MA: Harvard University press, 1938.

Lev, B. and Zarowin. P. The Boundaries of Financial Reporting and How to Extend Them, *Journal of Accounting Research(supplement)*, Vol.37, autumn, 1999, pp.353 − 385.

Ou, J. A, and S. H. Penman, Financial Statement Analysis and the Prediction of Stock Returns, *Journal of Accounting and Economics*, pp.299 − 329, 1993.

Penman, S. H. An Evaluation of accounting Rate − of − Return, *Journal of Accounting*, 1991, pp.233 − 256.

Rajgopal Shivaram and Suresh kotha and mohan Venkatachalam, *The Relevance of web Traffic for Stock Prices of Internet Firms University Of Washington*, Oct. 2000.

R. G. Mc Grath & I. C. Mac Millan, Assessing Technology Projects Using Real Options Reasoning: The STAR Approach, *Research Technology Management*(July/August), 2000.

S. P. Pratt and R. F. Reilly and R. P Schweihs, *A Business 3rd Ed.* Irwin, 1996, p.29.

The definition mostly used for FMV in the U.S. Internal Revenue Service, pp.59 − 60.

Tom Copeland, Tim Koller, and Jack Muurrin, Dong Won Park, Kwang Jun Kim, Soon Poong Park, 『Business Valuation』, Kyung Moon Sa, 2005, p.380.

Zhang, G., Accounting Information, Capital Investment Decisions, and Equity

Valuation: Theory and Empirical Implications, *Journal of Accounting Research (Autumn)*: 2000, pp.271 − 295.

Zhang, X. F. Information Uncertainty and Analyst Forecast Behavior, *Contemporary Accounting Research* 23(2): 2006, pp.565 − 590.

Choi, W., S. Kwon., and J. Lobo, Market Valuation of Intangible Assets, *Journal of Business Research*(49), 1996, pp.34 − 45.

3. References e.t.c.

www.Venturestorm.com.

Appendix

The total of the Outlets in A Hotel

NPV Data Result

Classification			0		1		2		3		4		5		6		7		8		9		10
Estimated years		2007		2008		2009		2010		2011		2012		2013		2014		2015		2016		2017
Economic value added				−6,341,183		−5,938,468		−5,475,653		−5,152,890		−5,107,751		−5,111,405		−5,298,014		−5,452,976		−5,529,851		−5,523,062
Total cash flow of the firm				9,552,683		9,863,872		10,172,924		10,557,333		10,886,007		11,296,524		11,680,301		12,114,102		12,543,800		12,988,197
Intangible assets depreciation																						
Tangible assets depreciation				7,058,126		7,322,190		7,594,107		7,862,187		8,130,431		8,433,577		8,722,623		9,037,592		9,359,857		9,692,975
Retirement grants				2,494,557		2,541,682		2,578,817		2,695,146		2,755,577		2,862,946		2,957,678		3,076,511		3,183,943		3,295,222
Inflow of total cash flow of the firm				3,211,500		3,925,404		4,697,271		5,404,443		5,778,256		6,185,119		6,382,287		6,661,126		7,013,949		7,465,135
Increase of net working capital				11,377,797		12,013,322		12,936,942		14,087,131		14,132,775		14,303,014		12,897,805		13,106,969		13,353,994		13,545,519
Investment cash flow				−5,736,659		−5,736,659		−5,736,659		−5,736,659		−5,736,659		−5,736,659		−5,736,659		−5,736,659		−5,736,659		−5,736,659
Outflow of total cash flow of the firm				5,641,138		6,276,663		7,200,283		8,350,472		8,396,116		8,566,355		7,161,146		7,370,310		7,617,335		7,808,860
Free cash flow				−2,429,638		−2,351,259		−2,503,013		−2,946,029		−2,617,859		−2,381,237		−778,859		−709,184		−603,386		−343,725
Weighted average cost of capital	8.53%	1.00000		0.92143		0.84904		0.78234		0.72087		0.66424		0.61205		0.56396		0.51966		0.47883		0.44121
Discount cash flow method		0		−2,238,752		−1,996,316		−1,958,196		−2,123,707		−1,738,875		−1,457,434		−439,248		−368,531		−288,918		−151,654

DCF VALUE	−10,055,846
TERMINAL VALUE	−18,791,625
Net present vale (NPV)	−28,847,471

Terminal value 5 years by Growth Rate

1) NPV (w/5% growth)	
Growth rate	5.00%
terminal value	−47,707,202

2) NPV (w/no growth)	
Growth rate	0%
terminal value	−18,791,625

3) NPV (w/−5% growth)	
Growth rate	−5.00%
terminal value	−11253107

NPV Data Result by Terminal Value (5 years)			
	NPV(w/5% growth)	NPV(w/no growth)	NPV(w/−5% growth)
DCF VALUE	−10,055,846	−10,055,846	−10,055,846
TERMINAL VALUE	−47,707,202	−18,791,625	−11,253,107
NPV	−57,763,048	−28,847,471	−21,308,953

DCF VALUE	−12,761,631
TERMINAL VALUE	−1,638,890
NPV	−14,400,521

Terminal value 10 years by Growth Rate

1) NPV (w/5% growth)	
Growth rate	5.00%
terminal value	−4,160,729

2) NPV (w/no growth)	
Growth rate	0%
terminal value	−1,638,890

3) NPV (w/−5% growth)	
Growth rate	−5.00%
terminal value	−981,427

NPV Data Result by Terminal Value (10years)			
	NPV(w/5% growth)	NPV(w/no growth)	NPV(w/−5% growth)
DCF VALUE	−12,761,631	−12,761,631	−12,761,631
TERMINAL VALUE	−4,160,729	−1,638,890	−981,427
NPV	−16,922,360	−14,400,521	−13,743,058

The total of the Outlets in B Hotel

NPV Data Result

Classification		0	1	2	3	4	5	6	7	8	9	10
Estimated years		2007	2008	2009	2010	2011	2012	2013	2014	2015	2016	2017
Economic value added			1,148,923	1,575,183	2,362,735	3,796,589	6,187,323	10,172,062	15,199,350	23,211,759	36,063,154	56,486,156
Total cash flow of the firm			5,176,181	5,370,783	5,541,301	5,736,578	5,942,484	6,151,740	6,381,331	6,603,554	6,839,324	7,082,446
Intangible assets depreciation												
Tangible assets depreciation			4,178,254	4,359,501	4,528,598	4,680,076	4,887,477	5,054,973	5,244,221	5,415,009	5,609,924	5,811,002
Retirement grants			997,927	1,011,282	1,012,703	1,056,502	1,055,007	1,096,767	1,137,110	1,188,546	1,229,400	1,271,443
Inflow of total cash flow of the firm			6,325,104	6,945,966	7,904,036	9,533,167	12,129,807	16,323,802	21,580,681	29,815,313	42,902,478	63,568,602
Increase of net working capital			5,357,695	5,611,158	6,003,191	6,532,049	6,576,830	6,707,227	6,114,171	6,128,903	6,239,075	6,328,778
Investment cash flow			-3,495,464	-3,495,464	-3,495,464	-3,495,464	-3,495,464	-3,495,464	-3,495,464	-3,495,464	-3,495,464	-3,495,464
Outflow of total cash flow of the firm			1,862,231	2,115,694	2,507,727	3,036,584	3,081,366	3,211,762	2,618,707	2,633,439	2,743,611	2,833,314
Free cash flow			4,462,873	4,830,273	5,396,309	6,496,582	9,048,441	13,112,039	18,961,975	27,181,874	40,158,867	60,735,288
Weighted average cost of capital	8.53%	1.00000	0.92143	0.84904	0.78234	0.72087	0.66424	0.61205	0.56396	0.51966	0.47883	0.44121
Discount cash flow method		0	4,112,245	4,101,101	4,221,725	4,683,198	6,010,294	8,025,213	10,693,855	14,125,197	19,229,189	26,796,928

DCF VALUE	23,128,563
TERMINAL VALUE	64,951,876
NPV	88,080,439

Terminal value 5 years by Growth Rate

1) NPV (w/5% growth)	
Growth rate	5.00%
terminal value	164,896,446

2) NPV (w/no growth)	
Growth rate	0%
terminal value	64,951,876

3) NPV (w/-5% growth)	
Growth rate	-5.00%
terminal value	38,895,538

NPV Data Result by Terminal Value (5 years)			
	NPV(w/5% growth)	NPV(w/no growth)	NPV(w/-5% growth)
DCF VALUE	23,128,563	23,128,563	23,128,563
TERMINAL VALUE	164,896,446	64,951,876	38,895,538
NPV	188,025,009	88,080,439	62,024,101

DCF VALUE	101,998,945
TERMINAL VALUE	289,588,288
NPV	391,587,233

Terminal value 10 years by Growth Rate

1) NPV (w/5% growth)	
Growth rate	5.00%
terminal value	735,191,690

2) NPV (w/no growth)	
Growth rate	0%
terminal value	289,588,288

3) NPV (w/-5% growth)	
Growth rate	-5.00%
terminal value	173,415,964

NPV Data Result by Terminal Value (10 years)			
	NPV(w/5% growth)	NPV(w/no growth)	NPV(w/-5% growth)
DCF VALUE	101,998,945	101,998,945	101,998,945
TERMINAL VALUE	735,191,690	289,588,288	173,415,964
NPV	837,190,635	391,587,233	275,414,909

Deli Shop in A Hotel

NPV Data Result

Classification		0	1	2	3	4	5	6	7	8	9	10
Estimated years		2007	2008	2009	2010	2011	2012	2013	2014	2015	2016	2017
Economic value added			-53,526	-44,803	-36,493	-15,425	-8,893	-5,962	-4,699	-4,655	-3,526	-2,714
Total cash flow of the firm			159,096	164,274	170,169	178,684	183,315	190,133	195,470	203,398	210,609	218,084
Intangible assets depreciation												
Tangible assets depreciation			123,135	126,196	131,274	138,258	142,250	147,601	151,345	157,554	163,114	168,931
Retirement grants			35,961	38,078	38,895	40,425	41,066	42,532	44,126	45,844	47,495	49,153
Inflow of total cash flow of the firm			105,570	119,471	133,676	163,259	174,422	184,171	190,771	198,743	207,083	215,370
Increase of net working capital			278,926	296,111	321,023	347,817	352,052	356,129	319,323	324,483	330,991	335,974
Investment cash flow			-67,231	-67,231	-67,231	-67,231	-67,231	-67,231	-67,231	-67,231	-67,231	-67,231
Outflow of total cash flow of the firm			211,694	228,880	253,792	280,586	284,820	288,897	252,091	257,252	263,760	268,743
Free cash flow			-106,124	-109,409	-120,116	-117,327	-110,398	-104,726	-61,320	-58,509	-56,676	-53,373
Weighted average cost of capital	8.53%	1.00000	0.92143	0.84904	0.78234	0.72087	0.66424	0.61205	0.56396	0.51966	0.47883	0.44121
Discount cash flow method		0	-97,786	-92,893	-93,971	-84,578	-73,330	-64,098	-34,582	-30,404	-27,138	-23,549

DCF VALUE	-442,558
TERMNAL VALUE	-792,461
NPV	-1,235,019

Terminal value 5 years by Growth Rate

1) NPV (w/ 5% growth)

Growth rate	5.00%
terminal value	-2,011,858

2) NPV (w/ no growth)

Growth rate	0%
terminal value	-792,461

3) NPV (w/ -5% growth)

Growth rate	-5.00%
terminal value	-474,554

	NPV Data Result by Terminal Value (5 years)		
	NPV(w/ 5% growth)	NPV(w/ no growth)	NPV(w/ -5% growth)
DCF VALUE	-442,558	-442,558	-442,558
TERMNAL VALUE	-2,011,858	-792,461	-474,554
NPV	-2,454,416	-1,235,019	-917,112

DCF VALUE	-622,329
TERMNAL VALUE	-254,489
NPV	-876,818

Terminal value 10 years by Growth Rate

1) NPV (w/ 5% growth)

Growth rate	5.00%
terminal value	-646,083

2) NPV (w/ no growth)

Growth rate	0%
terminal value	-254,489

3) NPV (w/ -5% growth)

Growth rate	-5.00%
terminal value	-152,397

	NPV Data Result by Terminal Value (10 years)		
	NPV(w/ 5% growth)	NPV(w/ no growth)	NPV(w/ -5% growth)
DCF VALUE	-622,329	-622,329	-622,329
TERMNAL VALUE	-646,083	-254,489	-152,397
NPV	-1,268,412	-876,818	-774,726

Lounge Bar in A Hotel

NPV Data Result

Classification		0	1	2	3	4	5	6	7	8	9	10
Estimated years		2007	2008	2009	2010	2011	2012	2013	2014	2015	2016	2017
Economic value added			-122,142	112,257	358,215	410,253	393,701	355,604	252,325	322,686	433,833	457,933
Total cash flow of the firm			425,663	422,859	442,396	465,975	472,797	491,994	501,562	525,889	543,774	563,109
Intangible assets depreciation												
Tangible assets depreciation			352,942	347,604	364,629	384,694	389,482	405,807	412,560	433,366	447,969	463,908
Retirement grants			72,721	75,255	77,767	81,282	83,315	86,187	89,002	92,523	95,806	99,202
Inflow of total cash flow of the firm			303,521	535,116	800,611	876,228	866,498	847,598	753,887	848,575	977,607	1,021,042
Increase of net working capital			434,142	450,723	485,648	523,433	516,130	520,148	473,041	486,181	493,615	499,742
Investment cash flow			-121,529	-121,529	-121,529	-121,529	-121,529	-121,529	-121,529	-121,529	-121,529	-121,529
Outflow of total cash flow of the firm			312,613	329,194	364,119	401,904	394,601	398,619	351,512	364,652	372,086	378,213
Free cash flow			-9,092	205,923	436,492	474,324	471,897	448,979	402,375	483,924	605,521	642,829
Weighted average cost of capital	8.53%	1.00000	0.92143	0.84904	0.78234	0.72087	0.66424	0.61205	0.56396	0.51966	0.47883	0.44121
Discount cash flow method		0	-8,378	174,837	341,483	341,927	313,450	274,797	226,925	251,473	289,941	283,622

DCF VALUE	1,163,319
TERMNAL VALUE	3,387,383
NPV	4,550,702

Terminal value 5 years by Growth Rate

1) NPV(w/5% growth)

Growth rate	5.00%
terminal value	8,599,711

2) NPV(w/no growth)

Growth rate	0%
terminal value	3,387,383

3) NPV(w/-5% growth)

Growth rate	-5.00%
terminal value	2,028,488

	NPV Data Result by Terminal Value (5 years)		
	NPV(w/5% growth)	NPV(w/no growth)	NPV(w/-5% growth)
DCF VALUE	1,163,319	1,163,319	1,163,319
TERMNAL VALUE	8,599,711	3,387,383	2,028,488
NPV	9,763,030	4,550,702	3,191,807

DCF VALUE	2,490,077
TERMNAL VALUE	3,065,038
NPV	5,555,115

Terminal value 10 years by Growth Rate

1) NPV(w/5% growth)

Growth rate	5.00%
terminal value	7,781,360

2) NPV(w/no growth)

Growth rate	0%
terminal value	3,065,038

3) NPV(w/-5% growth)

Growth rate	-5.00%
terminal value	1835456

	NPV Data Result by Terminal Value (10 years)		
	NPV(w/5% growth)	NPV(w/no growth)	NPV(w/-5% growth)
DCF VALUE	2,490,077	2,490,077	2,490,077
TERMNAL VALUE	7,781,360	3,065,038	1,835,456
NPV	10,271,437	5,555,115	4,325,533

Room Service in A Hotel

NPV Data Result

Classification		0		1	2	3	4	5	6	7	8	9	10
Estimated years			2007	2008	2009	2010	2011	2012	2013	2014	2015	2016	2017
Economic value added				-177,631	-144,861	-118,140	-98,988	-95,302	-93,910	-81,994	-71,101	-62,556	-55,695
Total cash flow of the firm				304,016	301,551	305,585	322,168	320,002	335,226	342,574	360,394	372,509	385,296
Intangible assets depreciation													
Tangible assets depreciation				195,949	191,937	197,772	209,115	209,741	219,673	223,127	234,871	242,705	251,184
Retirement grants				108,066	109,614	107,813	113,053	110,261	115,553	119,446	125,522	129,804	134,112
Inflow of total cash flow of the firm				126,385	156,690	187,445	223,180	224,700	241,316	260,580	289,293	309,953	329,601
Increase of net working capital				176,377	186,986	197,270	213,977	209,937	211,264	192,206	198,288	201,418	203,480
Investment cash flow				-58,909	-58,909	-58,909	-58,909	-58,909	-58,909	-58,909	-58,909	-58,909	-58,909
Outflow of total cash flow of the firm				117,468	128,076	138,361	155,068	151,027	152,354	133,297	139,379	142,509	144,571
Free cash flow				8,917	28,613	49,084	68,113	73,673	88,961	127,282	149,914	167,444	185,030
Weighted average cost of capital	8.53%	1.00000		0.92143	0.84904	0.78234	0.72087	0.66424	0.61205	0.56396	0.51966	0.47883	0.44121
Discount cash flow method		0		8,217	24,294	38,400	49,100	48,936	54,449	71,783	77,904	80,177	81,637

DCF VALUE	168,947
TERMINAL VALUE	528,840
NPV	697,787

Terminal value 5 years by Growth Rate

1) NPV (w/5% growth)

Growth rate	5.00%
terminal value	1,342,592

2) NPV (w/no growth)

Growth rate	0%
terminal value	528,840

3) NPV (w/-5% growth)

Growth rate	-5.00%
terminal value	316,689

	NPV Data Result by Terminal Value (5 years)		
	NPV(w/5% growth)	NPV(w/no growth)	NPV(w/-5% growth)
DCF VALUE	168,947	168,947	168,947
TERMINAL VALUE	1,342,592	528,840	316,689
NPV	1,511,539	697,787	485,636

DCF VALUE	534,897
TERMINAL VALUE	882,232
NPV	1,417,129

Terminal value 10 years by Growth Rate

1) NPV (w/5% growth)

Growth rate	5.00%
terminal value	2,239,766

2) NPV (w/no growth)

Growth rate	0%
terminal value	882,232

3) NPV (w/-5% growth)

Growth rate	-5.00%
terminal value	528313

	NPV Data Result by Terminal Value (10 years)		
	NPV(w/5% growth)	NPV(w/no growth)	NPV(w/-5% growth)
DCF VALUE	534,897	534,897	534,897
TERMINAL VALUE	2,239,766	882,232	528,313
NPV	2,774,663	1,417,129	1,063,210

Western Restaurant 1(M) in A Hotel

NPV Data Result

Classification		0	1	2	3	4	5	6	7	8	9	10
Estimated years		2007	2008	2009	2010	2011	2012	2013	2014	2015	2016	2017
Economic value added			-779,778	-772,582	-749,605	-723,689	-714,652	-713,534	-701,585	-689,021	-675,932	-664,271
Total cash flow of the firm			586,961	609,176	627,276	651,302	672,985	698,316	722,634	748,547	775,269	802,730
Intangible assets depreciation												
Tangible assets depreciation			470,500	495,758	512,824	529,533	550,607	570,439	592,502	611,552	633,747	656,313
Retirement grants			116,461	113,418	114,452	121,770	122,378	127,877	130,132	136,994	141,522	146,418
Inflow of total cash flow of the firm			-192,817	-163,406	-122,329	-72,387	-41,667	-15,218	21,049	59,526	99,337	138,459
Increase of net working capital			298,239	310,871	329,600	355,623	350,725	354,403	314,630	330,584	335,205	338,681
Investment cash flow			-431,294	-431,294	-431,294	-431,294	-431,294	-431,294	-431,294	-431,294	-431,294	-431,294
Outflow of total cash flow of the firm			-133,055	-120,423	-101,694	-75,671	-80,569	-76,891	-116,664	-100,710	-96,089	-92,613
Free cash flow			-59,762	-42,983	-20,635	3,285	38,902	61,673	137,714	160,236	195,426	231,072
Weighted average cost of capital	8.53%	1.00000	0.92143	0.84904	0.78234	0.72087	0.66424	0.61205	0.56396	0.51966	0.47883	0.44121
Discount cash flow method		0	-55,067	-36,494	-16,144	2,368	25,840	37,747	77,665	83,267	93,575	101,951

DCF VALUE	-79,497
TERMINAL VALUE	279,247
NPV	199,750

Terminal value 5 years by Growth Rate

1) NPV (w/ 5% growth)	
Growth rate	5.00%
terminal value	708,938

2) NPV (w/ no growth)	
Growth rate	0%
terminal value	279,247

3) NPV (w/ -5% growth)	
Growth rate	-5.00%
terminal value	167,223

	NPV Data Result by Terminal Value (5 years)		
	NPV(w/ 5% growth)	NPV(w/ no growth)	NPV(w/ -5% growth)
DCF VALUE	-79,497	-79,497	-79,497
TERMINAL VALUE	708,938	279,247	167,223
NPV	629,441	199,750	87,726

DCF VALUE	314,708
TERMINAL VALUE	1,101,761
NPV	1,416,469

Terminal value 10 years by Growth Rate

1) NPV (w/ 5% growth)	
Growth rate	5.00%
terminal value	2,797,094

2) NPV (w/ no growth)	
Growth rate	0%
terminal value	1,101,761

3) NPV (w/ -5% growth)	
Growth rate	-5.00%
terminal value	659,775

	NPV Data Result by Terminal Value (10 years)		
	NPV(w/ 5% growth)	NPV(w/ no growth)	NPV(w/ -5% growth)
DCF VALUE	314,708	314,708	314,708
TERMINAL VALUE	2,797,094	1,101,761	659,775
NPV	3,111,802	1,416,469	974,483

Pub Style Bar in A Hotel

NPV Data Result

Classification		0	1	2	3	4	5	6	7	8	9	10
Estimated years		2007	2008	2009	2010	2011	2012	2013	2014	2015	2016	2017
Economic value added			-313,706	-228,100	-222,363	-202,885	-196,064	-194,468	-181,299	-166,119	-157,537	-148,677
Total cash flow of the firm			387,990	392,002	402,704	421,035	428,426	445,725	458,403	478,297	494,837	512,223
Intangible assets depreciation												
Tangible assets depreciation			257,106	259,612	267,784	278,611	284,077	295,732	303,854	317,167	328,091	339,649
Retirement grants			130,884	132,390	134,920	142,424	144,349	149,993	154,549	161,131	166,745	172,574
Inflow of total cash flow of the firm			74,284	163,902	180,341	218,150	232,362	251,257	277,104	312,178	337,300	363,546
Increase of net working capital			407,052	406,467	421,322	449,374	438,319	443,364	410,854	425,250	427,850	430,905
Investment cash flow			-155,920	-155,920	-155,920	-155,920	-155,920	-155,920	-155,920	-155,920	-155,920	-155,920
Outflow of total cash flow of the firm			251,132	250,548	265,402	293,454	282,399	287,444	254,934	269,330	271,930	274,985
Free cash flow			-176,849	-86,645	-85,061	-75,304	-50,037	-36,187	22,170	42,848	65,369	88,561
Weighted average cost of capital	8.53%	1.00000	0.92143	0.84904	0.78234	0.72087	0.66424	0.61205	0.56396	0.51966	0.47883	0.44121
Discount cash flow method		0	-162,954	-73,565	-66,546	-54,285	-33,236	-22,148	12,503	22,266	31,301	39,074

DCF VALUE	-390,586
TERMINAL VALUE	-359,174
NPV	-749,760

Terminal value 5 years by Growth Rate

1) NPV (w/5% growth)	
Growth rate	5.00%
terminal value	-911,852

2) NPV (w/no growth)	
Growth rate	0%
terminal value	-359,174

3) NPV (w/-5% growth)	
Growth rate	-5.00%
terminal value	-215,086

NPV Data Result by Terminal Value (5 years)			
	NPV(w/5% growth)	NPV(w/no growth)	NPV(w/-5% growth)
DCF VALUE	-390,586	-390,586	-390,586
TERMINAL VALUE	-911,852	-359,174	-215,086
NPV	-1,302,438	-749,760	-605,672

DCF VALUE	-307,590
TERMINAL VALUE	422,264
NPV	114,674

Terminal value 10 years by Growth Rate

1) NPV (w/5% growth)	
Growth rate	5.00%
terminal value	1,072,021

2) NPV (w/no growth)	
Growth rate	0%
terminal value	422,264

3) NPV (w/-5% growth)	
Growth rate	-5.00%
terminal value	252,867

NPV Data Result by Terminal Value (10 years)			
	NPV(w/5% growth)	NPV(w/no growth)	NPV(w/-5% growth)
DCF VALUE	-307,590	-307,590	-307,590
TERMINAL VALUE	1,072,021	422,264	252,867
NPV	764,431	114,674	-54,723

Buffet Restaurant in A Hotel

NPV Data Result

Classification		0	1	2	3	4	5	6	7	8	9	10
Estimated years		2007	2008	2009	2010	2011	2012	2013	2014	2015	2016	2017
Economic value added			-519,938	-479,631	-472,056	-451,394	-404,412	-394,118	-370,169	-350,098	-332,502	-313,905
Total cash flow of the firm			899,385	942,261	971,640	1,020,667	1,051,928	1,091,220	1,125,495	1,166,713	1,208,861	1,251,701
Intangible assets depreciation												
Tangible assets depreciation			572,799	595,816	615,994	648,539	664,230	689,635	709,401	737,441	763,847	790,880
Retirement grants			326,586	346,445	355,646	372,128	387,698	401,585	416,094	429,272	445,014	460,822
Inflow of total cash flow of the firm			379,447	462,630	499,584	569,273	647,516	697,102	755,326	816,615	876,359	937,796
Increase of net working capital			1,719,559	1,901,953	2,098,731	2,336,410	2,309,496	2,318,643	2,077,451	2,108,892	2,164,511	2,202,019
Investment cash flow			-418,314	-418,314	-418,314	-418,314	-418,314	-418,314	-418,314	-418,314	-418,314	-418,314
Outflow of total cash flow of the firm			1,301,245	1,483,639	1,680,417	1,918,095	1,891,182	1,900,328	1,659,137	1,690,578	1,746,197	1,783,705
Free cash flow			-921,798	-1,021,009	-1,180,832	-1,348,823	-1,243,666	-1,203,227	-903,811	-873,963	-869,838	-845,909
Weighted average cost of capital	8.53%	1.00000	0.92143	0.84904	0.78234	0.72087	0.66424	0.61205	0.56396	0.51966	0.47883	0.44121
Discount cash flow method		0	-849,376	-866,879	-923,807	-972,327	-826,087	-736,434	-509,716	-454,159	-416,503	-373,222

DCF VALUE	-4,438,476
TERMNAL VALUE	-8,927,334
NPV	-13,365,810

Terminal value 5 years by Growth Rate

1) NPV (w/ 5% growth)	
Growth rate	5.00%
terminal value	-22,664,251

2) NPV (w/ no growth)	
Growth rate	0%
terminal value	-8,927,334

3) NPV (w/ -5% growth)	
Growth rate	-5.00%
terminal value	-5,346,011

NPV Data Result by Terminal Value (5 years)			
	NPV(w/ 5% growth)	NPV(w/ no growth)	NPV(w/ -5% growth)
DCF VALUE	-4,438,476	-4,438,476	-4,438,476
TERMNAL VALUE	-22,664,251	-8,927,334	-5,346,011
NPV	-27,102,727	-13,365,810	-9,784,487

DCF VALUE	-6,928,510
TERMNAL VALUE	-4,033,325
NPV	-10,961,835

Terminal value 10 years by Growth Rate

1) NPV (w/ 5% growth)	
Growth rate	5.00%
terminal value	-10,239,596

2) NPV (w/ no growth)	
Growth rate	0%
terminal value	-4,033,325

3) NPV (w/ -5% growth)	
Growth rate	-5.00%
terminal value	-2,415,301

NPV Data Result by Terminal Value (10 years)			
	NPV(w/ 5% growth)	NPV(w/ no growth)	NPV(w/ -5% growth)
DCF VALUE	-6,928,510	-6,928,510	-6,928,510
TERMNAL VALUE	-10,239,596	-4,033,325	-2,415,301
NPV	-17,168,106	-10,961,835	-9,343,811

Western Restaurant 2 (C) in A Hotel

NPV Data Result

Classification		0		1	2	3	4	5	6	7	8	9	10
Estimated years			2007	2008	2009	2010	2011	2012	2013	2014	2015	2016	2017
Economic value added				-788,371	-777,978	-770,537	-763,955	-755,418	-741,992	-734,309	-725,364	-716,851	-708,168
Total cash flow of the firm				441,037	458,205	473,929	492,106	509,504	527,691	546,790	565,811	586,086	606,948
Intangible assets depreciation													
Tangible assets depreciation				319,812	336,106	347,648	359,536	373,444	387,116	401,601	414,818	429,835	445,131
Retirement grants				121,225	122,098	126,282	132,570	136,060	140,575	145,189	150,992	156,251	161,817
Inflow of total cash flow of the firm				-347,334	-319,773	-296,608	-271,849	-245,914	-214,301	-187,519	-159,553	-130,765	-101,220
Increase of net working capital				329,565	345,429	372,944	408,466	414,833	426,534	384,500	383,182	390,841	397,329
Investment cash flow				-269,272	-269,272	-269,272	-269,272	-269,272	-269,272	-269,272	-269,272	-269,272	-269,272
Outflow of total cash flow of the firm				60,293	76,158	103,672	139,195	145,561	157,263	115,228	113,910	121,569	128,057
Free cash flow				-407,627	-395,931	-400,280	-411,044	-391,476	-371,564	-302,747	-273,463	-252,334	-229,277
Weighted average cost of capital	8.53%	1.00000		0.92143	0.84904	0.78234	0.72087	0.66424	0.61205	0.56396	0.51966	0.47883	0.44121
Discount cash flow method		0		-375,601	-336,162	-313,153	-296,310	-260,032	-227,415	-170,738	-142,107	-120,825	-101,159

DCF VALUE	-1,581,258
TERMINAL VALUE	-2,810,107
NPV	-4,391,365

Terminal value 5 years by Growth Rate

1) NPV (w/ 5% growth)	
Growth rate	5.00%
terminal value	-7,134,152

2) NPV (w/ no growth)	
Growth rate	0%
terminal value	-2,810,107

3) NPV (w/ -5% growth)	
Growth rate	-5.00%
terminal value	-1,682,794

DCF VALUE	-2,343,502
TERMINAL VALUE	-1,093,202
NPV	-3,436,704

Terminal value 10 years by Growth Rate

1) NPV (w/ 5% growth)	
Growth rate	5.00%
terminal value	-2,775,365

2) NPV (w/ no growth)	
Growth rate	0%
terminal value	-1,093,202

3) NPV (w/ -5% growth)	
Growth rate	-5.00%
terminal value	-654,649

NPV Data Result by Terminal Value (5 years)		
NPV(w/ 5% growth)	NPV(w/ no growth)	NPV(w/ -5% growth)
DCF VALUE	-1,581,258	-1,581,258	-1,581,258
TERMINAL VALUE	-7,134,152	-2,810,107	-1,682,794
NPV	-8,715,410	-4,391,365	-3,264,052

NPV Data Result by Terminal Value (10 years)		
NPV(w/ 5% growth)	NPV(w/ no growth)	NPV(w/ -5% growth)
DCF VALUE	-2,343,502	-2,343,502	-2,343,502
TERMINAL VALUE	-2,775,365	-1,093,202	-654,649
NPV	-5,118,867	-3,436,704	-2,998,151

Banquet in A Hotel

NPV Data Result

Classification		0	1	2	3	4	5	6	7	8	9	10
Estimated years		2007	2008	2009	2010	2011	2012	2013	2014	2015	2016	2017
Economic value added			-46,605	-69,140	-83,417	-92,724	-100,514	-104,393	-112,901	-118,715	-125,514	-131,786
Total cash flow of the firm			3,502,784	3,685,940	3,816,974	3,946,372	4,098,906	4,245,937	4,405,527	4,550,991	4,715,816	4,883,799
Intangible assets depreciation												
Tangible assets depreciation			2,969,178	3,139,710	3,263,307	3,367,408	3,505,268	3,629,627	3,769,074	3,889,180	4,030,820	4,174,840
Retirement grants			533,606	546,230	553,667	578,964	593,638	616,310	636,453	661,811	684,996	708,959
Inflow of total cash flow of the firm			3,456,179	3,616,800	3,733,557	3,853,648	3,998,392	4,141,544	4,292,626	4,432,276	4,590,302	4,752,013
Increase of net working capital			4,159,044	4,506,712	4,877,117	5,327,968	5,385,205	5,467,528	4,904,914	4,946,927	5,059,482	5,138,449
Investment cash flow			-2,970,822	-2,970,822	-2,970,822	-2,970,822	-2,970,822	-2,970,822	-2,970,822	-2,970,822	-2,970,822	-2,970,822
Outflow of total cash flow of the firm			1,188,222	1,535,890	1,906,296	2,357,146	2,414,383	2,496,707	1,934,092	1,976,105	2,088,660	2,167,627
Free cash flow			2,267,957	2,080,910	1,827,262	1,496,502	1,584,009	1,644,837	2,358,534	2,456,171	2,501,642	2,584,386
Weighted average cost of capital	8.53%	1.00000	0.92143	0.84904	0.78234	0.72087	0.66424	0.61205	0.56396	0.51966	0.47883	0.44121
Discount cash flow method		0	2,089,774	1,766,778	1,429,532	1,078,785	1,052,155	1,006,721	1,330,126	1,276,362	1,197,856	1,140,253

DCF VALUE	7,417,024
TERMINAL VALUE	11,370,399
NPV	18,787,423

Terminal value 5 years by Growth Rate

1) NPV (w/ 5% growth)	
Growth rate	5.00%
terminal value	28,866,578

2) NPV (w/ no growth)	
Growth rate	0%
terminal value	11,370,399

3) NPV (w/ -5% growth)	
Growth rate	-5.00%
terminal value	6,809,007

	NPV Data Result by Terminal Value (5 years)		
	NPV(w/ 5% growth)	NPV(w/ no growth)	NPV(w/ -5% growth)
DCF VALUE	7,417,024	7,417,024	7,417,024
TERMINAL VALUE	28,866,578	11,370,399	6,809,007
NPV	36,283,602	18,787,423	14,226,031

DCF VALUE	13,368,342
TERMINAL VALUE	12,322,454
NPV	25,690,796

Terminal value 10 years by Growth Rate

1) NPV (w/ 5% growth)	
Growth rate	5.00%
terminal value	31,283,606

2) NPV (w/ no growth)	
Growth rate	0%
terminal value	12,322,454

3) NPV (w/ -5% growth)	
Growth rate	-5.00%
terminal value	7,379,132

	NPV Data Result by Terminal Value (10 years)		
	NPV(w/ 5% growth)	NPV(w/ no growth)	NPV(w/ -5% growth)
DCF VALUE	13,368,342	13,368,342	13,368,342
TERMINAL VALUE	31,283,606	12,322,454	7,379,132
NPV	44,651,948	25,690,796	20,747,474

Main Bar in A Hotel

NPV Data Result

Classification		0	1	2	3	4	5	6	7	8	9	10
Estimated years		2007	2008	2009	2010	2011	2012	2013	2014	2015	2016	2017
Economic value added			-221,766	-361,334	-378,030	-511,422	-686,369	-939,163	-1,366,949	-1,868,000	-2,469,627	-3,378,677
Total cash flow of the firm			107,228	107,321	111,425	115,905	117,942	122,693	126,320	131,753	136,283	141,105
Intangible assets depreciation												
Tangible assets depreciation			90,272	91,046	94,711	98,282	100,287	104,416	107,340	111,949	115,815	119,917
Retirement grants			16,956	16,275	16,714	17,624	17,655	18,278	18,980	19,804	20,468	21,188
Inflow of total cash flow of the firm			-114,538	-254,013	-266,605	-395,517	-568,427	-816,470	-1,240,629	-1,736,247	-2,333,344	-3,237,572
Increase of net working capital			143,397	144,030	153,585	162,799	157,755	160,367	147,141	152,725	154,057	155,490
Investment cash flow			-60,905	-60,905	-60,905	-60,905	-60,905	-60,905	-60,905	-60,905	-60,905	-60,905
Outflow of total cash flow of the firm			82,492	83,125	92,679	101,894	96,850	99,461	86,236	91,820	93,152	94,585
Free cash flow			-197,030	-337,138	-359,284	-497,411	-665,277	-915,931	-1,326,865	-1,828,067	-2,426,497	-3,332,157
Weighted average cost of capital	8.53%	1.00000	0.92143	0.84904	0.78234	0.72087	0.66424	0.61205	0.56396	0.51966	0.47883	0.44121
Discount cash flow method		0	-181,550	-286,244	-281,081	-358,569	-441,901	-560,595	-748,303	-949,964	-1,161,874	-1,470,176

DCF VALUE	-1,549,345
TERMNAL VALUE	-4,775,523
NPV	-6,324,868

Terminal value 5 years by Growth Rate

1) NPV (w/5% growth)

Growth rate	5.00%
terminal value	-12,123,850

2) NPV (w/no growth)

Growth rate	0%
terminal value	-4,775,523

3) NPV (w/-5% growth)

Growth rate	-5.00%
terminal value	-2,859,756

NPV Data Result by Terminal Value (5 years)			
	NPV(w/5% growth)	NPV(w/no growth)	NPV(w/-5% growth)
DCF VALUE	-1,549,345	-1,549,345	-1,549,345
TERMNAL VALUE	-12,123,850	-4,775,523	-2,859,756
NPV	-13,673,195	-6,324,868	-4,409,101

DCF VALUE	-6,440,257
TERMNAL VALUE	-15,887,857
NPV	-22,328,114

Terminal value 10 years by Growth Rate

1) NPV (w/5% growth)

Growth rate	5.00%
terminal value	-40,335,264

2) NPV (w/no growth)

Growth rate	0%
terminal value	-15,887,857

3) NPV (w/-5% growth)

Growth rate	-5.00%
terminal value	-9,514,224

NPV Data Result by Terminal Value (10 years)			
	NPV(w/5% growth)	NPV(w/no growth)	NPV(w/-5% growth)
DCF VALUE	-6,440,257	-6,440,257	-6,440,257
TERMNAL VALUE	-40,335,264	-15,887,857	-9,514,224
NPV	-46,775,521	-22,328,114	-15,954,481

Japanese Restaurant in A Hotel

NPV Data Result

Classification		0	1	2	3	4	5	6	7	8	9	10
Estimated years		2007	2008	2009	2010	2011	2012	2013	2014	2015	2016	2017
Economic value added			-985,319	-801,530	-627,539	-462,516	-305,316	-224,765	-168,713	-124,110	-88,642	-61,465
Total cash flow of the firm			622,193	652,972	668,898	702,539	716,289	744,293	770,087	798,474	827,403	856,410
Intangible assets depreciation												
Tangible assets depreciation			394,222	414,738	429,988	446,526	462,588	479,028	496,662	513,324	531,949	550,902
Retirement grants			227,972	238,234	238,910	256,013	253,701	265,265	273,425	285,150	295,454	305,509
Inflow of total cash flow of the firm			-363,126	-148,558	41,359	240,023	410,973	519,528	601,374	674,364	738,761	794,945
Increase of net working capital			702,092	754,464	831,033	925,281	909,464	907,742	818,359	835,491	854,547	868,845
Investment cash flow			-325,408	-325,408	-325,408	-325,408	-325,408	-325,408	-325,408	-325,408	-325,408	-325,408
Outflow of total cash flow of the firm			376,684	429,055	505,624	599,872	584,055	582,334	492,950	510,082	529,139	543,437
Free cash flow			-739,810	-577,614	-464,265	-359,849	-173,082	-62,806	108,423	164,282	209,622	251,509
Weighted average cost of capital	8.53%	1.00000	0.92143	0.84904	0.78234	0.72087	0.66424	0.61205	0.56396	0.51966	0.47883	0.44121
Discount cash flow method		0	-681,686	-490,418	-363,211	-259,405	-114,967	-38,440	61,147	85,370	100,373	110,968

DCF VALUE	-1,909,687
TERMINAL VALUE	-1,242,422
NPV	-3,152,109

Terminal value 5 years by Growth Rate

1) NPV(w/5% growth)

Growth rate	5.00%
terminal value	-3,154,197

2) NPV(w/no growth)

Growth rate	0%
terminal value	-1,242,422

3) NPV(w/-5% growth)

Growth rate	-5.00%
terminal value	-744,007

	NPV Data Result by Terminal Value (5 years)		
	NPV(w/5% growth)	NPV(w/no growth)	NPV(w/-5% growth)
DCF VALUE	-1,909,687	-1,909,687	-1,909,687
TERMINAL VALUE	-3,154,197	-1,242,422	-744,007
NPV	-5,063,884	-3,152,109	-2,653,694

DCF VALUE	-1,590,269
TERMINAL VALUE	1,199,206
NPV	-391,063

Terminal value 10 years by Growth Rate

1) NPV(w/5% growth)

Growth rate	5.00%
terminal value	3,044,481

2) NPV(w/no growth)

Growth rate	0%
terminal value	1,199,206

3) NPV(w/-5% growth)

Growth rate	-5.00%
terminal value	718,128

	NPV Data Result by Terminal Value (10 years)		
	NPV(w/5% growth)	NPV(w/no growth)	NPV(w/-5% growth)
DCF VALUE	-1,590,269	-1,590,269	-1,590,269
TERMINAL VALUE	3,044,481	1,199,206	718,128
NPV	1,454,212	-391,063	-872,141

Chinese Restaurant in A Hotel

NPV Data Result

Classification		0	1	2	3	4	5	6	7	8	9	10
Estimated years		2007	2008	2009	2010	2011	2012	2013	2014	2015	2016	2017
Economic value added			-105,002	-96,664	-80,499	-74,837	-68,226	-68,195	-61,554	-55,503	-50,174	-45,992
Total cash flow of the firm			477,115	497,350	513,784	532,474	551,513	571,768	591,501	612,632	634,549	657,096
Intangible assets depreciation												
Tangible assets depreciation			312,100	327,436	339,719	351,528	364,304	378,061	391,286	404,766	419,369	434,296
Retirement grants			165,015	169,914	174,066	180,946	187,210	193,707	200,216	207,866	215,181	222,799
Inflow of total cash flow of the firm			372,113	400,686	433,285	457,637	483,287	503,573	529,947	557,129	584,375	611,104
Increase of net working capital			723,976	781,999	860,254	941,320	949,249	970,119	868,830	870,821	891,799	907,485
Investment cash flow			-268,382	-268,382	-268,382	-268,382	-268,382	-268,382	-268,382	-268,382	-268,382	-268,382
Outflow of total cash flow of the firm			455,594	513,616	591,872	672,938	680,867	701,737	600,448	602,439	623,417	639,103
Free cash flow			-83,481	-112,930	-158,587	-215,301	-197,579	-198,164	-70,501	-45,309	-39,042	-27,999
Weighted average cost of capital	8.53%	1.00000	0.92143	0.84904	0.78234	0.72087	0.66424	0.61205	0.56396	0.51966	0.47883	0.44121
Discount cash flow method		0	-76,923	-95,882	-124,068	-155,205	-131,239	-121,286	-39,760	-23,545	-18,694	-12,353

DCF VALUE	-583,317
TERMINAL VALUE	-1,418,270
NPV	-2,001,587

Terminal value 5 years by Growth Rate

1) NPV (w/ 5% growth)	
Growth rate	5.00%
terminal value	-3,600,630

2) NPV (w/ no growth)	
Growth rate	0%
terminal value	-1,418,270

3) NPV (w/ -5% growth)	
Growth rate	-5.00%
terminal value	-849311

NPV Data Result by Terminal Value (5 years)			
	NPV(w/ 5% growth)	NPV(w/ no growth)	NPV(w/ -5% growth)
DCF VALUE	-583,317	-583,317	-583,317
TERMINAL VALUE	-3,600,630	-1,418,270	-849,311
NPV	-4,183,947	-2,001,587	-1,432,628

DCF VALUE	-798,955
TERMINAL VALUE	-133,496
NPV	-932,451

Terminal value 10 years by Growth Rate

1) NPV (w/ 5% growth)	
Growth rate	5.00%
terminal value	-338,913

2) NPV (w/ no growth)	
Growth rate	0%
terminal value	-133,496

3) NPV (w/ -5% growth)	
Growth rate	-5.00%
terminal value	-79,942

NPV Data Result by Terminal Value (10 years)			
	NPV(w/ 5% growth)	NPV(w/ no growth)	NPV(w/ -5% growth)
DCF VALUE	-798,955	-798,955	-798,955
TERMINAL VALUE	-338,913	-133,496	-79,942
NPV	-1,137,868	-932,451	-878,897

Korean Restaurant in A Hotel

NPV Data Result

Classification		0	1	2	3	4	5	6	7	8	9	10
Estimated years		2007	2008	2009	2010	2011	2012	2013	2014	2015	2016	2017
Economic value added			-569,273	-552,636	-543,878	-538,800	-505,184	-476,507	-451,290	-434,123	-416,829	-398,571
Total cash flow of the firm			416,107	434,645	447,770	467,508	479,944	497,695	514,568	533,733	552,895	572,430
Intangible assets depreciation												
Tangible assets depreciation			206,453	211,342	218,730	227,557	233,430	242,488	249,881	259,915	269,039	278,569
Retirement grants			209,654	223,303	229,040	239,952	246,513	255,207	264,687	273,818	283,856	293,861
Inflow of total cash flow of the firm			-153,166	-117,991	-96,108	-71,292	-25,240	21,188	63,278	99,610	136,066	173,859
Increase of net working capital			395,867	415,280	446,789	487,170	483,645	485,176	438,743	450,381	458,169	464,296
Investment cash flow			-144,028	-144,028	-144,028	-144,028	-144,028	-144,028	-144,028	-144,028	-144,028	-144,028
Outflow of total cash flow of the firm			251,839	271,252	302,761	343,142	339,617	341,148	294,715	306,353	314,141	320,268
Free cash flow			-405,005	-389,243	-398,869	-414,433	-364,858	-319,960	-231,438	-206,743	-178,075	-146,410
Weighted average cost of capital	8.53%	1.00000	0.92143	0.84904	0.78234	0.72087	0.66424	0.61205	0.56396	0.51966	0.47883	0.44121
Discount cash flow method		0	-373,186	-330,483	-312,049	-298,753	-242,351	-195,831	-130,522	-107,435	-85,267	-64,597

DCF VALUE	-1,556,822
TERMNAL VALUE	-2,619,032
NPV	-4,175,854

Terminal value 5 years by Growth Rate

1) NPV (w/5% growth)	
Growth rate	5.00%
terminal value	-6,649,062

2) NPV (w/no growth)	
Growth rate	0%
terminal value	-2,619,032

3) NPV (w/-5% growth)	
Growth rate	-5.00%
terminal value	-1,568,371

NPV Data Result by Terminal Value (5 years)			
	NPV(w/5% growth)	NPV(w/no growth)	NPV(w/-5% growth)
DCF VALUE	-1,556,822	-1,556,822	-1,556,822
TERMNAL VALUE	-6,649,062	-2,619,032	-1,568,371
NPV	-8,205,884	-4,175,854	-3,125,193

DCF VALUE	-2,140,474
TERMNAL VALUE	-698,085
NPV	-2,838,559

Terminal value 10 years by Growth Rate

1) NPV (w/5% growth)	
Growth rate	5.00%
terminal value	-1,772,262

2) NPV (w/no growth)	
Growth rate	0%
terminal value	-698,085

3) NPV (w/-5% growth)	
Growth rate	-5.00%
terminal value	-418,039

NPV Data Result by Terminal Value (10 years)			
	NPV(w/5% growth)	NPV(w/no growth)	NPV(w/-5% growth)
DCF VALUE	-2,140,474	-2,140,474	-2,140,474
TERMNAL VALUE	-1,772,262	-698,085	-418,039
NPV	-3,912,736	-2,838,559	-2,558,513

Western Restaurant 3 (S) in A Hotel

NPV Data Result

Classification		0	1	2	3	4	5	6	7	8	9	10
Estimated years		2007	2008	2009	2010	2011	2012	2013	2014	2015	2016	2017
Economic value added			-762,051	-722,241	-684,789	-634,477	-604,079	-597,810	-596,938	-573,050	-551,231	-531,526
Total cash flow of the firm			623,456	637,310	654,044	673,434	697,728	723,820	749,114	777,212	804,346	832,819
Intangible assets depreciation												
Tangible assets depreciation			433,773	448,098	464,337	478,172	496,797	514,867	532,838	552,015	571,548	591,929
Retirement grants			189,683	189,212	189,707	195,261	200,931	208,954	216,275	225,197	232,798	240,890
Inflow of total cash flow of the firm			-138,595	-84,931	-30,745	38,957	93,649	126,010	152,176	204,162	253,115	301,293
Increase of net working capital			702,377	717,901	750,909	804,974	840,733	848,639	763,792	775,618	786,081	795,821
Investment cash flow			-281,785	-281,785	-281,785	-281,785	-281,785	-281,785	-281,785	-281,785	-281,785	-281,785
Outflow of total cash flow of the firm			420,592	436,115	469,124	523,189	558,948	566,854	482,007	493,833	504,296	514,036
Free cash flow			-559,186	-521,046	-499,869	-484,233	-465,298	-440,844	-329,831	-289,671	-251,181	-212,743
Weighted average cost of capital	8.53%	1.00000	0.92143	0.84904	0.78234	0.72087	0.66424	0.61205	0.56396	0.51966	0.47883	0.44121
Discount cash flow method		0	-515,254	-442,390	-391,065	-349,069	-309,068	-269,818	-186,013	-150,529	-120,272	-93,864

DCF VALUE	-2,006,846
TERMINAL VALUE	-3,340,027
NPV	-5,346,873

Terminal value 5 years by Growth Rate

1) NPV (w/5% growth)	
Growth rate	5.00%
terminal value	-8,479,488

2) NPV (w/no growth)	
Growth rate	0%
terminal value	-3,340,027

3) NPV (w/-5% growth)	
Growth rate	-5.00%
terminal value	-2,000,129

NPV Data Result by Terminal Value (5 years)			
	NPV(w/5% growth)	NPV(w/no growth)	NPV(w/-5% growth)
DCF VALUE	-2,006,846	-2,006,846	-2,006,846
TERMINAL VALUE	-8,479,488	-3,340,027	-2,000,129
NPV	-10,486,334	-5,346,873	-4,006,975

DCF VALUE	-2,827,342
TERMINAL VALUE	-1,014,367
NPV	-3,841,709

Terminal value 10 years by Growth Rate

1) NPV (w/5% growth)	
Growth rate	5.00%
terminal value	-2,575,222

2) NPV (w/no growth)	
Growth rate	0%
terminal value	-1,014,367

3) NPV (w/-5% growth)	
Growth rate	-5.00%
terminal value	-607,440

NPV Data Result by Terminal Value (10 years)			
	NPV(w/5% growth)	NPV(w/no growth)	NPV(w/-5% growth)
DCF VALUE	-2,827,342	-2,827,342	-2,827,342
TERMINAL VALUE	-2,575,222	-1,014,367	-607,440
NPV	-5,402,564	-3,841,709	-3,434,782

Western Restaurant 4 (V) in A Hotel

NPV Data Result

Classification		0	1	2	3	4	5	6	7	8	9	10
Estimated years		2007	2008	2009	2010	2011	2012	2013	2014	2015	2016	2017
Economic value added			-481,706	-459,721	-449,860	-449,463	-431,586	-389,364	-379,894	-373,724	-363,824	-351,267
Total cash flow of the firm			339,633	352,000	364,328	378,134	390,217	405,210	418,362	433,943	449,385	465,337
Intangible assets depreciation												
Tangible assets depreciation			203,019	209,994	217,907	225,879	232,459	241,474	249,276	258,746	267,930	277,441
Retirement grants			136,615	142,006	146,421	152,256	157,759	163,735	169,086	175,197	181,455	187,896
Inflow of total cash flow of the firm			-142,073	-107,721	-85,532	-71,329	-41,369	15,846	38,468	60,219	85,561	114,070
Increase of net working capital			499,151	549,958	606,406	659,476	649,903	657,075	592,547	602,074	616,777	626,323
Investment cash flow			-161,292	-161,292	-161,292	-161,292	-161,292	-161,292	-161,292	-161,292	-161,292	-161,292
Outflow of total cash flow of the firm			337,859	388,666	445,113	498,184	488,610	495,783	431,255	440,782	455,485	465,030
Free cash flow			-479,932	-496,387	-530,646	-569,513	-529,979	-479,938	-392,787	-380,563	-369,924	-350,961
Weighted average cost of capital	8.53%	1.00000	0.92143	0.84904	0.78234	0.72087	0.66424	0.61205	0.56396	0.51966	0.47883	0.44121
Discount cash flow method		0	-442,226	-421,453	-415,143	-410,545	-352,031	-293,746	-221,517	-197,761	-177,130	-154,847

DCF VALUE	-2,041,398
TERMINAL VALUE	-3,804,319
NPV	-5,845,717

Terminal value 5 years by Growth Rate

1) NPV (w/ 5% growth)	
Growth rate	5.00%
terminal value	-9,658,207

2) NPV (w/ no growth)	
Growth rate	0%
terminal value	-3,804,319

3) NPV (w/ -5% growth)	
Growth rate	-5.00%
terminal value	-2,278,164

NPV Data Result by Terminal Value (5 years)			
	NPV(w/ 5% growth)	NPV(w/ no growth)	NPV(w/ -5% growth)
DCF VALUE	-2,041,398	-2,041,398	-2,041,398
TERMINAL VALUE	-9,658,207	-3,804,319	-2,278,164
NPV	-11,699,605	-5,845,717	-4,319,562

DCF VALUE	-3,086,399
TERMINAL VALUE	-1,673,396
NPV	-4,759,795

Terminal value 10 years by Growth Rate

1) NPV (w/ 5% growth)	
Growth rate	5.00%
terminal value	-4,248,331

2) NPV (w/ no growth)	
Growth rate	0%
terminal value	-1,673,396

3) NPV (w/ -5% growth)	
Growth rate	-5.00%
terminal value	-1,002,090

NPV Data Result by Terminal Value (10 years)			
	NPV(w/ 5% growth)	NPV(w/ no growth)	NPV(w/ -5% growth)
DCF VALUE	-3,086,399	-3,086,399	-3,086,399
TERMINAL VALUE	-4,248,331	-1,673,396	-1,002,090
NPV	-7,334,730	-4,759,795	-4,088,489

Deli Shop in B Hotel

NPV Data Result

Classification		0		1	2	3	4	5	6	7	8	9	10
Estimated years			2007	2008	2009	2010	2011	2012	2013	2014	2015	2016	2017
Economic value added				-178,328	227,472	-346,440	-312,994	-243,247	-166,185	35,109	-8,016	-4,112	-4,009
Total cash flow of the firm				75,041	78,217	80,702	84,918	85,455	88,622	91,771	95,434	98,869	102,334
Intangible assets depreciation													
Tangible assets depreciation				48,979	49,876	52,492	53,974	56,233	57,857	59,987	62,189	64,363	66,695
Retirement grants				26,062	28,341	28,210	30,944	29,222	30,765	31,784	33,244	34,506	35,638
Inflow of total cash flow of the firm				-103,287	305,689	-265,738	-228,076	-157,792	-77,563	126,880	87,418	94,757	98,325
Increase of net working capital				142,501	148,343	158,266	170,288	168,487	170,151	160,892	159,847	162,325	164,322
Investment cash flow				-15,451	-15,451	-15,451	-15,451	-15,451	-15,451	-15,451	-15,451	-15,451	-15,451
Outflow of total cash flow of the firm				127,050	132,892	142,815	154,837	153,036	154,700	145,440	144,396	146,874	148,871
Free cash flow				-230,337	172,797	-408,553	-382,912	-310,828	-232,263	-18,561	-56,978	-52,117	-50,546
Weighted average cost of capital	8.53%	1.00000		0.92143	0.84904	0.78234	0.72087	0.66424	0.61205	0.56396	0.51966	0.47883	0.44121
Discount cash flow method		0		-212,241	146,712	-319,626	-276,031	-206,463	-142,156	-10,468	-29,609	-24,955	-22,302

DCF VALUE	-867,649
TERMINAL VALUE	-2,231,199
NPV	-3,098,848

Terminal value 5 years by Growth Rate

1) NPV(w/5% growth)	
Growth rate	5.00%
terminal value	-5,664,451

2) NPV(w/no growth)	
Growth rate	0%
terminal value	-2,231,199

3) NPV(w/-5% growth)	
Growth rate	-5.00%
terminal value	-1,336,123

NPV Data Result by Terminal Value (5 years)			
	NPV(w/5% growth)	NPV(w/no growth)	NPV(w/-5% growth)
DCF VALUE	-867,649	-867,649	-867,649
TERMINAL VALUE	-5,664,451	-2,231,199	-1,336,123
NPV	-6,532,100	-3,098,848	-2,203,772

DCF VALUE	-1,097,139
TERMINAL VALUE	-241,013
NPV	-1,338,152

Terminal value 10 years by Growth Rate

1) NPV(w/5% growth)	
Growth rate	5.00%
terminal value	-611,870

2) NPV(w/no growth)	
Growth rate	0%
terminal value	-241,013

3) NPV(w/-5% growth)	
Growth rate	-5.00%
terminal value	-144,327

NPV Data Result by Terminal Value (10 years)			
	NPV(w/5% growth)	NPV(w/no growth)	NPV(w/-5% growth)
DCF VALUE	-1,097,139	-1,097,139	-1,097,139
TERMINAL VALUE	-611,870	-241,013	-144,327
NPV	-1,709,009	-1,338,152	-1,241,466

Buffet Restaurant in B Hotel

NPV Data Result

Classification		0	1	2	3	4	5	6	7	8	9	10
Estimated years		2007	2008	2009	2010	2011	2012	2013	2014	2015	2016	2017
Economic value added			-101,247	-104,890	-113,192	-131,311	-156,561	-188,944	-210,825	-237,439	-273,467	-318,151
Total cash flow of the firm			916,595	978,344	1,006,075	1,048,679	1,093,361	1,137,124	1,177,706	1,213,344	1,258,165	1,302,780
Intangible assets depreciation													
Tangible assets depreciation			717,864	771,069	796,471	827,606	869,341	902,785	936,504	962,509	998,333	1,033,970
Retirement grants			198,731	207,275	209,604	221,073	224,020	234,339	241,203	250,834	259,832	268,810
Inflow of total cash flow of the firm			815,348	873,454	892,883	917,368	936,800	948,180	966,881	975,905	984,698	984,629
Increase of net working capital			959,451	1,034,841	1,133,821	1,249,315	1,296,174	1,371,185	1,212,650	1,179,634	1,211,089	1,236,267
Investment cash flow			-657,555	-657,555	-657,555	-657,555	-657,555	-657,555	-657,555	-657,555	-657,555	-657,555
Outflow of total cash flow of the firm			301,896	377,286	476,266	591,760	638,619	713,630	555,095	522,079	553,534	578,712
Free cash flow			513,452	496,168	416,617	325,608	298,181	234,550	411,786	453,826	431,164	405,917
Weighted average cost of capital	8.53%	1.00000	0.92143	0.84904	0.78234	0.72087	0.66424	0.61205	0.56396	0.51966	0.47883	0.44121
Discount cash flow method		0	473,112	421,267	325,934	234,721	198,062	143,556	232,232	235,833	206,453	179,094

DCF VALUE	1,653,096
TERMINAL VALUE	2,140,411
NPV	3,793,507

Terminal value 5 years by Growth Rate

1) NPV (w/ 5% growth)	
Growth rate	5.00%
terminal value	5,433,964

2) NPV (w/ no growth)	
Growth rate	0%
terminal value	2,140,411

3) NPV (w/ -5% growth)	
Growth rate	-5.00%
terminal value	1,281,756

NPV Data Result by Terminal Value (5 years)			
	NPV(w/ 5% growth)	NPV(w/ no growth)	NPV(w/ -5% growth)
DCF VALUE	1,653,096	1,653,096	1,653,096
TERMINAL VALUE	5,433,964	2,140,411	1,281,756
NPV	7,087,060	3,793,507	2,934,852

DCF VALUE	2,650,264
TERMINAL VALUE	1,935,428
NPV	4,585,692

Terminal value 10 years by Growth Rate

1) NPV (w/ 5% growth)	
Growth rate	5.00%
terminal value	4,913,564

2) NPV (w/ no growth)	
Growth rate	0%
terminal value	1,935,428

3) NPV (w/ -5% growth)	
Growth rate	-5.00%
terminal value	1,159,004

NPV Data Result by Terminal Value (10 years)			
	NPV(w/ 5% growth)	NPV(w/ no growth)	NPV(w/ -5% growth)
DCF VALUE	2,650,264	2,650,264	2,650,264
TERMINAL VALUE	4,913,564	1,935,428	1,159,004
NPV	7,563,828	4,585,692	3,809,268

Lounge Bar in B Hotel

NPV Data Result

Classification		0		1	2	3	4	5	6	7	8	9	10
Estimated years			2007	2008	2009	2010	2011	2012	2013	2014	2015	2016	2017
Economic value added				21,789	-6,073	-11,058	-12,506	-13,212	-13,661	-14,431	-14,745	-15,311	-15,858
Total cash flow of the firm				290,772	306,515	317,115	325,711	341,316	351,569	367,148	378,025	391,750	405,792
Intangible assets depreciation													
Tangible assets depreciation				261,522	277,059	288,619	295,786	310,340	319,428	333,780	343,400	355,936	368,754
Retirement grants				29,250	29,457	28,496	29,926	30,976	32,141	33,368	34,625	35,814	37,038
Inflow of total cash flow of the firm				312,561	300,442	306,057	313,205	328,104	337,908	352,717	363,280	376,439	389,934
Increase of net working capital				232,581	239,149	254,907	276,217	275,470	281,604	267,480	261,059	265,127	268,838
Investment cash flow				-258,566	-258,566	-258,566	-258,566	-258,566	-258,566	-258,566	-258,566	-258,566	-258,566
Outflow of total cash flow of the firm				-25,984	-19,416	-3,659	17,651	16,905	23,038	8,914	2,493	6,561	10,272
Free cash flow				338,545	319,859	309,715	295,554	311,199	314,870	343,803	360,788	369,878	379,662
Weighted average cost of capital	8.53%		1.00000	0.92143	0.84904	0.78234	0.72087	0.66424	0.61205	0.56396	0.51966	0.47883	0.44121
Discount cash flow method		0		311,947	271,573	242,301	213,056	206,710	192,716	193,892	187,485	177,108	167,510

DCF VALUE	1,245,587
TERMINAL VALUE	2,233,868
NPV	3,479,455

Terminal value 5 years by Growth Rate

1) NPV (w/5% growth)	
Growth rate	5.00%
terminal value	5,671,227

2) NPV (w/no growth)	
Growth rate	0%
terminal value	2,233,868

3) NPV (w/-5% growth)	
Growth rate	-5.00%
terminal value	1,337,721

NPV Data Result by Terminal Value (5 years)			
	NPV(w/5% growth)	NPV(w/no growth)	NPV(w/-5% growth)
DCF VALUE	1,245,587	1,245,587	1,245,587
TERMINAL VALUE	5,671,227	2,233,868	1,337,721
NPV	6,916,814	3,479,455	2,583,308

DCF VALUE	2,164,298
TERMINAL VALUE	1,810,242
NPV	3,974,540

Terminal value 10 years by Growth Rate

1) NPV (w/5% growth)	
Growth rate	5.00%
terminal value	4,595,749

2) NPV (w/no growth)	
Growth rate	0%
terminal value	1,810,242

3) NPV (w/-5% growth)	
Growth rate	-5.00%
terminal value	1,084,039

NPV Data Result by Terminal Value (10 years)			
	NPV(w/5% growth)	NPV(w/no growth)	NPV(w/-5% growth)
DCF VALUE	2,164,298	2,164,298	2,164,298
TERMINAL VALUE	4,595,749	1,810,242	1,084,039
NPV	6,760,047	3,974,540	3,248,337

Room Service in B Hotel

NPV Data Result

Classification		0	1	2	3	4	5	6	7	8	9	10
Estimated years		2007	2008	2009	2010	2011	2012	2013	2014	2015	2016	2017
Economic value added			−27,004	−20,927	−15,376	−11,675	−10,841	−9,360	−6,826	−4,572	−2,911	−1,515
Total cash flow of the firm			102,704	102,920	105,528	108,583	111,137	115,247	119,408	124,316	128,561	133,089
Intangible assets depreciation												
Tangible assets depreciation			68,574	70,983	73,345	76,255	79,078	82,070	84,852	87,830	90,968	94,205
Retirement grants			34,129	31,936	32,182	32,328	32,059	33,177	34,555	36,486	37,592	38,884
Inflow of total cash flow of the firm			75,700	81,993	90,152	96,908	100,296	105,887	112,582	119,744	125,650	131,574
Increase of net working capital			49,587	49,123	50,759	54,847	55,183	56,488	51,192	52,454	52,864	53,398
Investment cash flow			−59,460	−59,460	−59,460	−59,460	−59,460	−59,460	−59,460	−59,460	−59,460	−59,460
Outflow of total cash flow of the firm			−9,873	−10,337	−8,701	−4,613	−4,277	−2,973	−8,268	−7,006	−6,597	−6,062
Free cash flow			85,573	92,330	98,853	101,521	104,574	108,860	120,850	126,750	132,247	137,636
Weighted average cost of capital	8.53%	1.00000	0.92143	0.84904	0.78234	0.72087	0.66424	0.61205	0.56396	0.51966	0.47883	0.44121
Discount cash flow method		0	78,850	78,392	77,336	73,184	69,461	66,628	68,155	65,866	63,323	60,726

DCF VALUE	377,223
TERMINAL VALUE	750,649
NPV	1,127,872

Terminal value 5 years by Growth Rate

1) NPV (w/5% growth)

Growth rate	5.00%
terminal value	1,905,709

2) NPV (w/no growth)

Growth rate	0%
terminal value	750,649

3) NPV (w/−5% growth)

Growth rate	−5.00%
terminal value	449,516

NPV Data Result by Terminal Value (5 years)	NPV(w/5% growth)	NPV(w/no growth)	NPV(w/−5% growth)
DCF VALUE	377,223	377,223	377,223
TERMINAL VALUE	1,905,709	750,649	449,516
NPV	2,282,932	1,127,872	826,739

DCF VALUE	701,921
TERMINAL VALUE	656,252
NPV	1,358,173

Terminal value 10 years by Growth Rate

1) NPV (w/5% growth)

Growth rate	5.00%
terminal value	1,666,059

2) NPV (w/no growth)

Growth rate	0%
terminal value	656,252

3) NPV (w/−5% growth)

Growth rate	−5.00%
terminal value	392,988

NPV Data Result by Terminal Value (10 years)	NPV(w/5% growth)	NPV(w/no growth)	NPV(w/−5% growth)
DCF VALUE	701,921	701,921	701,921
TERMINAL VALUE	1,666,059	656,252	392,988
NPV	2,367,980	1,358,173	1,094,909

Banquet in B Hotel

NPV Data Result

Classification		0	1	2	3	4	5	6	7	8	9	10
Estimated years		2007	2008	2009	2010	2011	2012	2013	2014	2015	2016	2017
Economic value added			5,904,999	10,143,058	20,247,986	44,787,281	98,729,774	136,970,123	134,210,045	99,910,082	58,306,246	20,341,115
Total cash flow of the firm			1,891,843	1,969,504	2,036,719	2,113,305	2,197,453	2,277,726	2,358,806	2,438,520	2,526,130	2,616,175
Intangible assets depreciation												
Tangible assets depreciation			1,609,957	1,679,822	1,745,006	1,806,940	1,888,941	1,956,548	2,026,198	2,092,296	2,167,687	2,245,381
Retirement grants			281,886	289,682	291,713	306,365	308,512	321,178	332,607	346,224	358,443	370,795
Inflow of total cash flow of the firm			7,796,842	12,112,562	22,284,705	46,900,586	100,927,227	139,247,849	136,568,851	102,348,602	60,832,376	22,957,290
Increase of net working capital			2,513,772	2,666,597	2,872,197	3,139,439	3,208,577	3,280,454	2,935,783	2,945,260	3,006,901	3,055,516
Investment cash flow			-1,309,429	-1,309,429	-1,309,429	-1,309,429	-1,309,429	-1,309,429	-1,309,429	-1,309,429	-1,309,429	-1,309,429
Outflow of total cash flow of the firm			1,204,343	1,357,168	1,562,768	1,830,010	1,899,148	1,971,025	1,626,354	1,635,831	1,697,472	1,746,087
Free cash flow			6,592,499	10,755,394	20,721,937	45,070,576	99,028,079	137,276,823	134,942,497	100,712,771	59,134,904	21,211,203
Weighted average cost of capital	8.53%	1.00000	0.92143	0.84904	0.78234	0.72087	0.66424	0.61205	0.56396	0.51966	0.47883	0.44121
Discount cash flow method		0	6,074,555	9,131,773	16,211,512	32,490,072	65,777,946	84,020,172	76,102,597	52,335,897	28,315,446	9,358,564

DCF VALUE	129,685,858
TERMINAL VALUE	710,847,257
NPV	840,533,115

Terminal value 5 years by Growth Rate

1) NPV (w/5% growth)	
Growth rate	5.00%
terminal value	1,804,662,059

2) NPV (w/ no growth)	
Growth rate	0%
terminal value	710,847,257

3) NPV (w/ -5% growth)	
Growth rate	-5.00%
terminal value	425,681,105

NPV Data Result by Terminal Value (5 years)			
	NPV(w/5% growth)	NPV(w/ no growth)	NPV(w/ -5% growth)
DCF VALUE	129,685,858	129,685,858	129,685,858
TERMINAL VALUE	1,804,662,059	710,847,257	425,681,105
NPV	1,934,347,917	840,533,115	555,366,963

DCF VALUE	379,818,534
TERMINAL VALUE	101,135,866
NPV	480,954,400

Terminal value 10 years by Growth Rate

1) NPV (w/5% growth)	
Growth rate	5.00%
terminal value	256,758,479

2) NPV (w/ no growth)	
Growth rate	0%
terminal value	101,135,866

3) NPV (w/ -5% growth)	
Growth rate	-5.00%
terminal value	60,563,823

NPV Data Result by Terminal Value (10 years)			
	NPV(w/5% growth)	NPV(w/ no growth)	NPV(w/ -5% growth)
DCF VALUE	379,818,534	379,818,534	379,818,534
TERMINAL VALUE	256,758,479	101,135,866	60,563,823
NPV	636,577,013	480,954,400	440,382,357

Chinese Restaurant in B Hotel

NPV Data Result

Classification		0	1	2	3	4	5	6	7	8	9	10
Estimated years		2007	2008	2009	2010	2011	2012	2013	2014	2015	2016	2017
Economic value added			-94,880	-75,635	-66,238	-60,090	-49,570	-34,898	-29,209	-24,879	-21,767	-19,221
Total cash flow of the firm			328,990	356,324	369,560	374,964	395,357	405,228	427,171	437,509	453,776	470,104
Intangible assets depreciation												
Tangible assets depreciation			244,846	268,662	281,141	284,561	303,395	310,307	327,572	334,288	346,905	359,527
Retirement grants			84,144	87,662	88,418	90,403	91,962	94,922	99,599	103,221	106,871	110,577
Inflow of total cash flow of the firm			234,110	280,689	303,322	314,874	345,787	370,330	397,962	412,630	432,009	450,883
Increase of net working capital			299,316	314,584	337,477	367,523	371,758	381,321	372,728	349,244	356,377	362,347
Investment cash flow			-284,617	-284,617	-284,617	-284,617	-284,617	-284,617	-284,617	-284,617	-284,617	-284,617
Outflow of total cash flow of the firm			14,700	29,967	52,861	82,906	87,142	96,704	88,111	64,627	71,760	77,730
Free cash flow			219,411	250,722	250,461	231,968	258,645	273,626	309,850	348,003	360,249	373,153
Weighted average cost of capital	8.53%	1.00000	0.92143	0.84904	0.78234	0.72087	0.66424	0.61205	0.56396	0.51966	0.47883	0.44121
Discount cash flow method		0	202,173	212,873	195,945	167,219	171,801	167,473	174,744	180,841	172,497	164,638

DCF VALUE	950,011
TERMINAL VALUE	1,856,614
NPV	2,806,625

Terminal value 5 years by Growth Rate

1) NPV (w/ 5% growth)	
Growth rate	5.00%
terminal value	4,713,476

2) NPV (w/ no growth)	
Growth rate	0%
terminal value	1,856,614

3) NPV (w/ -5% growth)	
Growth rate	-5.00%
terminal value	1,111,808

	NPV Data Result by Terminal Value (5 years)		
	NPV(w/ 5% growth)	NPV(w/ no growth)	NPV(w/ -5% growth)
DCF VALUE	950,011	950,011	950,011
TERMINAL VALUE	4,713,476	1,856,614	1,111,808
NPV	5,663,487	2,806,625	2,061,819

DCF VALUE	1,810,204
TERMINAL VALUE	1,779,205
NPV	3,589,409

Terminal value 10 years by Growth Rate

1) NPV (w/ 5% growth)	
Growth rate	5.00%
terminal value	4,516,954

2) NPV (w/ no growth)	
Growth rate	0%
terminal value	1,779,205

3) NPV (w/ -5% growth)	
Growth rate	-5.00%
terminal value	1,065,453

	NPV Data Result by Terminal Value (10 years)		
	NPV(w/ 5% growth)	NPV(w/ no growth)	NPV(w/ -5% growth)
DCF VALUE	1,810,204	1,810,204	1,810,204
TERMINAL VALUE	4,516,954	1,779,205	1,065,453
NPV	6,327,158	3,589,409	2,875,657

Pub Style Bar in B Hotel

NPV Data Result

Classification		0	1	2	3	4	5	6	7	8	9	10
Estimated years		2007	2008	2009	2010	2011	2012	2013	2014	2015	2016	2017
Economic value added			-129,897	-108,862	-98,061	-92,079	-89,754	-87,412	-52,898	-29,571	-10,627	4,885
Total cash flow of the firm			1,141,840	885,390	933,513	991,532	1,031,448	1,105,066	1,132,169	1,171,326	1,205,305	1,249,327
Intangible assets depreciation												
Tangible assets depreciation			1,057,818	821,539	866,511	919,468	957,235	1,024,993	1,050,865	1,086,770	1,118,362	1,159,235
Retirement grants			84,021	63,851	67,002	72,064	74,213	80,073	81,303	84,556	86,943	90,092
Inflow of total cash flow of the firm			1,011,943	776,528	835,452	899,453	941,694	1,017,654	1,079,271	1,141,755	1,194,678	1,254,212
Increase of net working capital			470,734	1,217,758	1,522,198	1,382,051	1,274,053	1,349,015	1,381,829	1,346,737	1,337,909	1,353,873
Investment cash flow			-901,931	-901,931	-901,931	-901,931	-901,931	-901,931	-901,931	-901,931	-901,931	-901,931
Outflow of total cash flow of the firm			1,372,666	315,827	620,266	480,120	372,122	447,084	479,898	444,806	435,978	451,941
Free cash flow			-360,723	460,701	215,186	419,333	569,572	570,570	599,372	696,949	758,700	802,270
Weighted average cost of capital	8.53%	1.00000	0.92143	0.84904	0.78234	0.72087	0.66424	0.61205	0.56396	0.51966	0.47883	0.44121
Discount cash flow method		0	-332,383	391,154	168,348	302,285	378,330	349,217	338,024	362,173	363,287	353,968

DCF VALUE	907,734
TERMINAL VALUE	4,088,526
NPV	4,996,260

Terminal value 5 years by Growth Rate

1) NPV (w/ 5% growth)

Growth rate	5.00%
terminal value	10,379,737

2) NPV (w/ no growth)

Growth rate	0%
terminal value	4,088,526

3) NPV (w/ -5% growth)

Growth rate	-5.00%
terminal value	2,448,358

	NPV Data Result by Terminal Value (5 years)		
	NPV(w/ 5% growth)	NPV(w/ no growth)	NPV(w/ -5% growth)
DCF VALUE	907,734	907,734	907,734
TERMINAL VALUE	10,379,737	4,088,526	2,448,358
NPV	11,287,471	4,996,260	3,356,092

DCF VALUE	2,674,403
TERMINAL VALUE	3,825,251
NPV	6,499,654

Terminal value 10 years by Growth Rate

1) NPV (w/ 5% growth)

Growth rate	5.00%
terminal value	9,711,349

2) NPV (w/ no growth)

Growth rate	0%
terminal value	3,825,251

3) NPV (w/ -5% growth)

Growth rate	-5.00%
terminal value	2,290,699

	NPV Data Result by Terminal Value (10 years)		
	NPV(w/ 5% growth)	NPV(w/ no growth)	NPV(w/ -5% growth)
DCF VALUE	2,674,403	2,674,403	2,674,403
TERMINAL VALUE	9,711,349	3,825,251	2,290,699
NPV	12,385,752	6,499,654	4,965,102

The total of the Food Outlets in A Hotel

NPV Data Result

Classification		0	1	2	3	4	5	6	7	8	9	10
Estimated years		2007	2008	2009	2010	2011	2012	2013	2014	2015	2016	2017
Economic value added			-4,013,752	-3,714,759	-3,459,535	-3,219,533	-2,931,644	-2,746,963	-2,596,705	-2,471,580	-2,354,252	-2,242,773
Total cash flow of the firm			4,405,888	4,583,919	4,721,670	4,918,164	5,070,109	5,260,013	5,438,551	5,637,065	5,838,794	6,045,472
Intangible assets depreciation													
Tangible assets depreciation			2,912,677	3,039,289	3,147,146	3,267,268	3,377,859	3,503,109	3,623,447	3,752,578	3,887,264	4,025,460
Retirement grants			1,493,211	1,544,630	1,574,523	1,650,896	1,692,250	1,756,904	1,815,104	1,884,486	1,951,530	2,020,012
Inflow of total cash flow of the firm			392,136	869,160	1,262,135	1,698,631	2,138,465	2,513,050	2,841,846	3,165,485	3,484,542	3,802,699
Increase of net working capital			5,370,827	5,777,854	6,296,665	6,918,720	6,908,047	6,968,332	6,258,852	6,357,043	6,497,930	6,600,798
Investment cash flow			-269,272	-269,272	-269,272	-269,272	-269,272	-269,272	-269,272	-269,272	-269,272	-269,272
Outflow of total cash flow of the firm			5,101,556	5,508,582	6,027,393	6,649,448	6,638,775	6,699,060	5,989,581	6,087,771	6,228,659	6,331,527
Free cash flow			-4,709,419	-4,639,423	-4,765,258	-4,950,817	-4,500,310	-4,186,011	-3,147,735	-2,922,286	-2,744,117	-2,528,828
Weighted average cost of capital	8.53%	1.00000	0.92143	0.84904	0.78234	0.72087	0.66424	0.61205	0.56396	0.51966	0.47883	0.44121
Discount cash flow method		0	-4,339,420	-3,939,061	-3,728,032	-3,568,901	-2,989,265	-2,562,045	-1,775,206	-1,518,581	-1,313,960	-1,115,741

DCF VALUE	-18,564,679
TERMINAL VALUE	-32,304,305
NPV	-50,868,984

Terminal value 5 years by Growth Rate

1) NPV (w/ 5% growth)	
Growth rate	5.00%
terminal value	-82,012,490

2) NPV (w/ no growth)	
Growth rate	0%
terminal value	-32,304,305

3) NPV (w/ -5% growth)	
Growth rate	-5.00%
terminal value	-19,344,989

NPV Data Result by Terminal Value (5 years)			
	NPV(w/5% growth)	NPV(w/no growth)	NPV(w/-5% growth)
DCF VALUE	-18,564,679	-18,564,679	-18,564,679
TERMINAL VALUE	-82,012,490	-32,304,305	-19,344,989
NPV	-100,577,169	-50,868,984	-37,909,668

DCF VALUE	-26,850,212
TERMINAL VALUE	-12,057,558
NPV	-38,907,770

Terminal value 10 years by Growth Rate

1) NPV (w/ 5% growth)	
Growth rate	5.00%
terminal value	-30,611,103

2) NPV (w/ no growth)	
Growth rate	0%
terminal value	-12,057,558

3) NPV (w/ -5% growth)	
Growth rate	-5.00%
terminal value	-7,220,503

NPV Data Result by Terminal Value (10 years)			
	NPV(w/5% growth)	NPV(w/no growth)	NPV(w/-5% growth)
DCF VALUE	-26,850,212	-26,850,212	-26,850,212
TERMINAL VALUE	-30,611,103	-12,057,558	-7,220,503
NPV	-57,461,315	-38,907,770	-34,070,715

The total of the Beverage Outlets in A Hotel

NPV Data Result

Classification		0		1	2	3	4	5	6	7	8	9	10
Estimated years		2007		2008	2009	2010	2011	2012	2013	2014	2015	2016	2017
Economic value added				-748,646	-787,862	-826,457	-886,477	-886,580	-921,493	-935,224	-982,450	-1,017,623	-1,053,521
Total cash flow of the firm				920,881	922,182	956,526	1,002,915	1,019,165	1,060,413	1,086,285	1,135,940	1,174,893	1,216,437
Intangible assets depreciation													
Tangible assets depreciation				700,320	698,262	727,124	761,586	773,846	805,955	823,755	862,482	891,875	923,474
Retirement grants				220,561	223,920	229,402	241,329	245,319	254,457	262,531	273,457	283,019	292,963
Inflow of total cash flow of the firm				172,235	134,320	130,069	116,438	132,585	138,920	151,061	153,490	157,270	162,916
Increase of net working capital				984,592	2,052,835	2,264,471	2,130,298	2,020,312	2,116,979	2,133,015	2,100,151	2,092,614	2,110,690
Investment cash flow				-60,905	-60,905	-60,905	-60,905	-60,905	-60,905	-60,905	-60,905	-60,905	-60,905
Outflow of total cash flow of the firm				923,687	1,991,929	2,203,566	2,069,393	1,959,407	2,056,074	2,072,110	2,039,246	2,031,709	2,049,785
Free cash flow				-751,452	-1,857,609	-2,073,497	-1,952,954	-1,826,822	-1,917,154	-1,921,048	-1,885,756	-1,874,439	-1,886,869
Weighted average cost of capital	8.53%	1.00000		0.92143	0.84904	0.78234	0.72087	0.66424	0.61205	0.56396	0.51966	0.47883	0.44121
Discount cash flow method		0		-692,414	-1,577,187	-1,622,171	-1,407,828	-1,213,440	-1,173,393	-1,083,401	-979,943	-897,534	-832,503

DCF VALUE	-6,513,040
TERMINAL VALUE	-13,113,369
NPV	-19,626,409

Terminal value 5 years by Growth Rate

1) NPV (w/5% growth)	
Growth rate	5.00%
terminal value	-33,291,540

2) NPV (w/no growth)	
Growth rate	0%
terminal value	-13,113,369

3) NPV (w/-5% growth)	
Growth rate	-5.00%
terminal value	-7,852,761

NPV Data Result by Terminal Value (5 years)			
	NPV(w/5% growth)	NPV(w/no growth)	NPV(w/-5% growth)
DCF VALUE	-6,513,040	-6,513,040	-6,513,040
TERMINAL VALUE	-33,291,540	-13,113,369	-7,852,761
NPV	-39,804,580	-19,626,409	-14,365,801

DCF VALUE	-11,479,814
TERMINAL VALUE	-8,996,670
NPV	-20,476,484

Terminal value 10 years by Growth Rate

1) NPV (w/5% growth)	
Growth rate	5.00%
terminal value	-22,840,278

2) NPV (w/no growth)	
Growth rate	0%
terminal value	-8,996,670

3) NPV (w/-5% growth)	
Growth rate	-5.00%
terminal value	-5,387,532

NPV Data Result by Terminal Value (10 years)			
	NPV(w/5% growth)	NPV(w/no growth)	NPV(w/-5% growth)
DCF VALUE	-11,479,814	-11,479,814	-11,479,814
TERMINAL VALUE	-22,840,278	-8,996,670	-5,387,532
NPV	-34,320,092	-20,476,484	-16,867,346

The total of the Other Outlets in A Hotel

NPV Data Result

Classification		0	1	2	3	4	5	6	7	8	9	10
Estimated years		2007	2008	2009	2010	2011	2012	2013	2014	2015	2016	2017
Economic value added			-231,157	-189,664	-154,633	-114,413	-104,195	-99,873	-86,693	-75,756	-66,083	-58,409
Total cash flow of the firm			463,112	465,825	475,754	500,852	503,317	525,359	538,044	563,792	583,118	603,380
Intangible assets depreciation												
Tangible assets depreciation			319,085	318,133	329,046	347,374	351,991	367,274	374,472	392,425	405,819	420,115
Retirement grants			144,027	147,692	146,708	153,478	151,327	158,085	163,572	171,367	177,299	183,265
Inflow of total cash flow of the firm			231,955	276,161	321,121	386,439	399,122	425,486	451,351	488,036	517,035	544,971
Increase of net working capital			455,303	483,097	518,294	561,794	561,988	567,392	511,529	522,771	532,409	539,454
Investment cash flow			-58,909	-58,909	-58,909	-58,909	-58,909	-58,909	-58,909	-58,909	-58,909	-58,909
Outflow of total cash flow of the firm			396,394	424,187	459,384	502,884	503,079	508,483	452,620	463,862	473,500	480,545
Free cash flow			-164,438	-148,027	-138,264	-116,446	-103,957	-82,997	-1,269	24,174	43,535	64,426
Weighted average cost of capital	8.53%	1.00000	0.92143	0.84904	0.78234	0.72087	0.66424	0.61205	0.56396	0.51966	0.47883	0.44121
Discount cash flow method		0	-151,519	-125,681	-108,169	-83,942	-69,052	-50,798	-716	12,562	20,846	28,425

DCF VALUE	-538,363
TERMINAL VALUE	-746,229
NPV	-1,284,592

Terminal value 5 years by Growth Rate

1) NPV (w/5% growth)	
Growth rate	5.00%
terminal value	-1,894,488

2) NPV (w/no growth)	
Growth rate	0%
terminal value	-746,229

3) NPV (w/-5% growth)	
Growth rate	-5.00%
terminal value	-446,869

NPV Data Result by Terminal Value (5 years)			
	NPV(w/5% growth)	NPV(w/no growth)	NPV(w/-5% growth)
DCF VALUE	-538,363	-538,363	-538,363
TERMINAL VALUE	-1,894,488	-746,229	-446,869
NPV	-2,432,851	-1,284,592	-985,232

DCF VALUE	-528,044
TERMINAL VALUE	307,182
NPV	-220,862

Terminal value 10 years by Growth Rate

1) NPV (w/5% growth)	
Growth rate	5.00%
terminal value	779,859

2) NPV (w/no growth)	
Growth rate	0%
terminal value	307,182

3) NPV (w/-5% growth)	
Growth rate	-5.00%
terminal value	183,952

NPV Data Result by Terminal Value (10 years)			
	NPV(w/5% growth)	NPV(w/no growth)	NPV(w/-5% growth)
DCF VALUE	-528,044	-528,044	-528,044
TERMINAL VALUE	779,859	307,182	183,952
NPV	251,815	-220,862	-344,092

The total of the Food Outlets in B Hotel

NPV Data Result

Classification		0	1	2	3	4	5	6	7	8	9	10
Estimated years		2007	2008	2009	2010	2011	2012	2013	2014	2015	2016	2017
Economic value added			-368,276	-367,615	-372,052	-390,566	-415,538	-441,055	-466,318	-494,389	-536,026	-586,739
Total cash flow of the firm			1,245,585	1,334,668	1,375,635	1,423,643	1,488,718	1,542,352	1,604,877	1,650,853	1,711,941	1,772,884
Intangible assets depreciation												
Tangible assets depreciation			962,710	1,039,731	1,077,612	1,112,167	1,172,736	1,213,092	1,264,075	1,296,797	1,345,238	1,393,497
Retirement grants			282,876	294,937	298,023	311,476	315,982	329,261	340,802	354,056	366,703	379,387
Inflow of total cash flow of the firm			877,309	967,053	1,003,583	1,033,077	1,073,180	1,101,297	1,138,559	1,156,464	1,175,915	1,186,145
Increase of net working capital			1,258,767	1,349,425	1,471,299	1,616,838	1,667,933	1,752,506	1,585,378	1,528,878	1,567,465	1,598,614
Investment cash flow			-269,272	-269,272	-269,272	-269,272	-269,272	-269,272	-269,272	-269,272	-269,272	-269,272
Outflow of total cash flow of the firm			989,495	1,080,153	1,202,027	1,347,567	1,398,661	1,483,234	1,316,106	1,259,606	1,298,193	1,329,342
Free cash flow			-112,186	-113,100	-198,444	-314,489	-325,481	-381,937	-177,547	-103,142	-122,279	-143,197
Weighted average cost of capital	8.53%	1.00000	0.92143	0.84904	0.78234	0.72087	0.66424	0.61205	0.56396	0.51966	0.47883	0.44121
Discount cash flow method		0	-103,372	-96,027	-155,250	-226,706	-216,196	-233,764	-100,130	-53,598	-58,550	-63,180

DCF VALUE	-797,551
TERMNAL VALUE	-2,336,381
NPV	-3,133,932

Terminal value 5 years by Growth Rate

1) NPV(w/5% growth)	
Growth rate	5.00%
terminal value	-5,931,482

2) NPV(w/no growth)	
Growth rate	0%
terminal value	-2,336,381

3) NPV(w/-5% growth)	
Growth rate	-5.00%
terminal value	-1,399,110

NPV Data Result by Terminal Value (5 years)			
	NPV(w/5% growth)	NPV(w/no growth)	NPV(w/-5% growth)
DCF VALUE	-797,551	-797,551	-797,551
TERMNAL VALUE	-5,931,482	-2,336,381	-1,399,110
NPV	-6,729,033	-3,133,932	-2,196,661

DCF VALUE	-1,306,773
TERMNAL VALUE	-682,772
NPV	-1,989,545

Terminal value 10 years by Growth Rate

1) NPV(w/5% growth)	
Growth rate	5.00%
terminal value	-1,733,386

2) NPV(w/no growth)	
Growth rate	0%
terminal value	-682,772

3) NPV(w/-5% growth)	
Growth rate	-5.00%
terminal value	-408,869

NPV Data Result by Terminal Value (10 years)			
	NPV(w/5% growth)	NPV(w/no growth)	NPV(w/-5% growth)
DCF VALUE	-1,306,773	-1,306,773	-1,306,773
TERMNAL VALUE	-1,733,386	-682,772	-408,869
NPV	-3,040,159	-1,989,545	-1,715,642

The total of the Beverage Outlets in B Hotel

NPV Data Result

Classification		0	1	2	3	4	5	6	7	8	9	10
Estimated years		2007	2008	2009	2010	2011	2012	2013	2014	2015	2016	2017
Economic value added			−14,714	151,904	249,603	206,939	164,709	74,841	244,186	373,384	499,318	638,826
Total cash flow of the firm			1,486,985	1,534,457	1,587,199	1,640,602	1,699,064	1,758,539	1,823,081	1,888,151	1,955,127	2,024,750
Intangible assets depreciation												
Tangible assets depreciation			1,369,712	1,415,943	1,466,935	1,514,818	1,569,864	1,624,110	1,684,585	1,744,039	1,806,021	1,870,420
Retirement grants			117,272	118,514	120,264	125,784	129,199	134,429	138,496	144,111	149,105	154,329
Inflow of total cash flow of the firm			1,472,271	1,686,361	1,836,802	1,847,541	1,863,773	1,833,380	2,067,267	2,261,535	2,454,445	2,663,576
Increase of net working capital			880,022	915,296	977,307	1,056,998	1,050,028	1,065,070	974,459	988,454	1,003,945	1,016,609
Investment cash flow			−269,272	−269,272	−269,272	−269,272	−269,272	−269,272	−269,272	−269,272	−269,272	−269,272
Outflow of total cash flow of the firm			610,750	646,024	708,035	787,726	780,756	795,798	705,188	719,183	734,673	747,337
Free cash flow			861,520	1,040,337	1,128,766	1,059,815	1,083,016	1,037,582	1,362,079	1,542,352	1,719,772	1,916,239
Weighted average cost of capital	8.53%	1.00000	0.92143	0.84904	0.78234	0.72087	0.66424	0.61205	0.56396	0.51966	0.47883	0.44121
Discount cash flow method		0	793,834	883,289	883,074	763,990	719,378	635,051	768,162	801,491	823,475	845,461

DCF VALUE	4,043,565
TERMNAL VALUE	7,774,154
NPV	11,817,719

Terminal value 5 years by Growth Rate

1) NPV (w/ 5% growth)	
Growth rate	5.00%
terminal value	19,736,618

2) NPV (w/ no growth)	
Growth rate	0%
terminal value	7,774,154

3) NPV (w/ −5% growth)	
Growth rate	−5.00%
terminal value	4,655,445

	NPV Data Result by Terminal Value (5 years)		
	NPV(w/ 5% growth)	NPV(w/ no growth)	NPV(w/ −5% growth)
DCF VALUE	4,043,565	4,043,565	4,043,565
TERMNAL VALUE	19,736,618	7,774,154	4,655,445
NPV	23,780,183	11,817,719	8,699,010

DCF VALUE	7,917,205
TERMNAL VALUE	9,136,704
NPV	17,053,909

Terminal value 10 years by Growth Rate

1) NPV (w/ 5% growth)	
Growth rate	5.00%
terminal value	23,195,789

2) NPV (w/ no growth)	
Growth rate	0%
terminal value	9,136,704

3) NPV (w/ −5% growth)	
Growth rate	−5.00%
terminal value	5,471,390

	NPV Data Result by Terminal Value (10 years)		
	NPV(w/ 5% growth)	NPV(w/ no growth)	NPV(w/ −5% growth)
DCF VALUE	7,917,205	7,917,205	7,917,205
TERMNAL VALUE	23,195,789	9,136,704	5,471,390
NPV	31,112,994	17,053,909	13,388,595

The total of the Other Outlets in B Hotel

NPV Data Result

Classification		0	1	2	3	4	5	6	7	8	9	10
Estimated years		2007	2008	2009	2010	2011	2012	2013	2014	2015	2016	2017
Economic value added			-227,961	183,365	-385,726	-349,214	-279,428	-201,779	1,032	-40,838	-36,264	-35,802
Total cash flow of the firm			177,744	181,137	186,229	193,501	196,592	203,869	211,178	219,750	227,430	235,422
Intangible assets depreciation												
Tangible assets depreciation			117,554	120,859	125,838	130,230	135,311	139,927	144,839	150,019	155,332	160,900
Retirement grants			60,191	60,277	60,392	63,271	61,281	63,942	66,339	69,730	72,098	74,522
Inflow of total cash flow of the firm			-50,217	364,502	-199,497	-155,713	-82,836	2,090	212,210	178,912	191,166	199,620
Increase of net working capital			192,089	197,466	209,025	225,135	223,670	226,639	212,084	212,301	215,189	217,720
Investment cash flow			-269,272	-269,272	-269,272	-269,272	-269,272	-269,272	-269,272	-269,272	-269,272	-269,272
Outflow of total cash flow of the firm			-77,183	-71,806	-60,247	-44,137	-45,602	-42,633	-57,188	-56,971	-54,083	-51,551
Free cash flow			26,967	436,307	-139,250	-111,576	-37,234	44,723	269,398	235,882	245,249	251,172
Weighted average cost of capital	8.53%	1.00000	0.92143	0.84904	0.78234	0.72087	0.66424	0.61205	0.56396	0.51966	0.47883	0.44121
Discount cash flow method		0	24,848	370,443	-108,940	-80,432	-24,732	27,373	151,931	122,578	117,432	110,819

DCF VALUE	181,187
TERMNAL VALUE	-267,273
NPV	-86,086

Terminal value 5 years by Growth Rate

1) NPV (w/ 5% growth)	
Growth rate	5.00%
terminal value	-678,539

2) NPV (w/ no growth)	
Growth rate	0%
terminal value	-267,273

3) NPV (w/ -5% growth)	
Growth rate	-5.00%
terminal value	-160,053

NPV Data Result by Terminal Value (5 years)	NPV(w/5% growth)	NPV(w/no growth)	NPV(w/-5% growth)
DCF VALUE	181,187	181,187	181,187
TERMNAL VALUE	-678,539	-267,273	-160,053
NPV	-497,352	-86,086	21,134

DCF VALUE	711,320
TERMNAL VALUE	1,197,596
NPV	1,908,916

Terminal value 10 years by Growth Rate

1) NPV (w/ 5% growth)	
Growth rate	5.00%
terminal value	3,040,394

2) NPV (w/ no growth)	
Growth rate	0%
terminal value	1,197,596

3) NPV (w/ -5% growth)	
Growth rate	-5.00%
terminal value	717,164

NPV Data Result by Terminal Value (10 years)	NPV(w/5% growth)	NPV(w/no growth)	NPV(w/-5% growth)
DCF VALUE	711,320	711,320	711,320
TERMNAL VALUE	3,040,394	1,197,596	717,164
NPV	3,751,714	1,908,916	1,428,484

The total of the Asian Restaurants in A Hotel

NPV Data Result

Classification		0	1	2	3	4	5	6	7	8	9	10
Estimated years		2007	2008	2009	2010	2011	2012	2013	2014	2015	2016	2017
Economic value added			-1,609,644	-1,398,781	-1,197,875	-1,019,630	-820,327	-709,170	-619,097	-549,072	-488,652	-436,641
Total cash flow of the firm			1,515,415	1,584,967	1,630,452	1,702,521	1,747,747	1,813,756	1,876,156	1,944,839	2,014,847	2,085,936
Intangible assets depreciation												
Tangible assets depreciation			912,774	953,516	988,437	1,025,610	1,060,322	1,099,578	1,137,828	1,178,005	1,220,356	1,263,766
Retirement grants			602,641	631,451	642,016	676,911	687,424	714,178	738,328	766,834	794,491	822,170
Inflow of total cash flow of the firm			-94,229	186,186	432,577	682,891	927,420	1,104,586	1,257,059	1,395,767	1,526,195	1,649,295
Increase of net working capital			1,821,936	1,951,742	2,138,076	2,353,771	2,342,358	2,363,038	2,125,932	2,156,693	2,204,516	2,240,626
Investment cash flow			-269,272	-269,272	-269,272	-269,272	-269,272	-269,272	-269,272	-269,272	-269,272	-269,272
Outflow of total cash flow of the firm			1,552,664	1,682,471	1,868,804	2,084,499	2,073,086	2,093,766	1,856,661	1,887,421	1,935,244	1,971,354
Free cash flow			-1,646,893	-1,496,284	-1,436,227	-1,401,607	-1,145,666	-989,180	-599,602	-491,654	-409,048	-322,059
Weighted average cost of capital	8.53%	1.00000	0.92143	0.84904	0.78234	0.72087	0.66424	0.61205	0.56396	0.51966	0.47883	0.44121
Discount cash flow method		0	-1,517,504	-1,270,407	-1,123,611	-1,010,378	-760,992	-605,427	-338,153	-255,491	-195,864	-142,095

DCF VALUE	-5,682,892
TERMINAL VALUE	-8,223,867
NPV	-13,906,759

Terminal value 5 years by Growth Rate

1) NPV (w/ 5% growth)	
Growth rate	5.00%
terminal value	-20,878,326

2) NPV (w/ no growth)	
Growth rate	0%
terminal value	-8,223,867

3) NPV (w/ -5% growth)	
Growth rate	-5.00%
terminal value	-4,924,750

NPV Data Result by Terminal Value (5 years)			
	NPV(w/ 5% growth)	NPV(w/ no growth)	NPV(w/ -5% growth)
DCF VALUE	-5,682,892	-5,682,892	-5,682,892
TERMINAL VALUE	-20,878,326	-8,223,867	-4,924,750
NPV	-26,561,218	-13,906,759	-10,607,642

DCF VALUE	-7,219,922
TERMINAL VALUE	-1,535,588
NPV	-8,755,510

Terminal value 10 years by Growth Rate

1) NPV (w/ 5% growth)	
Growth rate	5.00%
terminal value	-3,898,472

2) NPV (w/ no growth)	
Growth rate	0%
terminal value	-1,535,588

3) NPV (w/ -5% growth)	
Growth rate	-5.00%
terminal value	-919,566

NPV Data Result by Terminal Value (10 years)			
	NPV(w/ 5% growth)	NPV(w/ no growth)	NPV(w/ -5% growth)
DCF VALUE	-7,219,922	-7,219,922	-7,219,922
TERMINAL VALUE	-3,898,472	-1,535,588	-919,566
NPV	-11,118,394	-8,755,510	-8,139,488

The total of the Western Restaurants in A Hotel

NPV Data Result

Classification			0	1	2	3	4	5	6	7	8	9	10
Estimated years		2007	2008	2009	2010	2011	2012	2013	2014	2015	2016	2017
Economic value added				−3,180,104	−3,053,219	−2,962,046	−2,850,926	−2,732,158	−2,652,771	−2,592,387	−2,514,074	−2,436,033	−2,357,542
Total cash flow of the firm				2,890,473	2,998,952	3,091,217	3,215,643	3,322,362	3,446,257	3,562,395	3,692,225	3,823,946	3,959,535
Intangible assets depreciation													
Tangible assets depreciation				1,999,903	2,085,773	2,158,710	2,241,658	2,317,537	2,403,531	2,485,619	2,574,573	2,666,907	2,761,693
Retirement grants				890,570	913,179	932,507	973,985	1,004,825	1,042,726	1,076,776	1,117,652	1,157,039	1,197,842
Inflow of total cash flow of the firm				−289,631	−54,267	129,171	364,717	590,204	793,486	970,008	1,178,151	1,387,913	1,601,993
Increase of net working capital				3,548,892	3,826,112	4,158,589	4,564,950	4,565,689	4,605,294	4,132,920	4,200,349	4,293,415	4,360,172
Investment cash flow				−269,272	−269,272	−269,272	−269,272	−269,272	−269,272	−269,272	−269,272	−269,272	−269,272
Outflow of total cash flow of the firm				3,279,620	3,556,840	3,889,317	4,295,678	4,296,418	4,336,023	3,863,648	3,931,078	4,024,143	4,090,901
Free cash flow				−3,569,251	−3,611,107	−3,760,146	−3,930,961	−3,706,213	−3,542,537	−2,893,640	−2,752,926	−2,636,230	−2,488,907
Weighted average cost of capital	8.53%	1.00000	0.92143	0.84904	0.78234	0.72087	0.66424	0.61205	0.56396	0.51966	0.47883	0.44121
Discount cash flow method			0	−3,288,830	−3,065,979	−2,941,697	−2,833,716	−2,461,798	−2,168,207	−1,631,906	−1,430,572	−1,262,300	−1,098,127

DCF VALUE	−14,592,020
TERMINAL VALUE	−26,604,089
NPV	−41,196,109

Terminal value 5 years by Growth Rate

1) NPV(w/5% growth)	
Growth rate	5.00%
terminal value	−67,541,079

2) NPV(w/no growth)	
Growth rate	0%
terminal value	−26,604,089

3) NPV(w/−5% growth)	
Growth rate	−5.00%
terminal value	−15,931,493

	NPV Data Result by Terminal Value (5 years)		
	NPV(w/5% growth)	NPV(w/no growth)	NPV(w/−5% growth)
DCF VALUE	−14,592,020	−14,592,020	−14,592,020
TERMINAL VALUE	−67,541,079	−26,604,089	−15,931,493
NPV	−82,133,099	−41,196,109	−30,523,513

DCF VALUE	−22,183,132
TERMINAL VALUE	−11,867,208
NPV	−34,050,340

Terminal value 10 years by Growth Rate

1) NPV(w/5% growth)	
Growth rate	5.00%
terminal value	−30,127,851

2) NPV(w/no growth)	
Growth rate	0%
terminal value	−11,867,208

3) NPV(w/−5% growth)	
Growth rate	−5.00%
terminal value	−7,106,514

	NPV Data Result by Terminal Value (10 years)		
	NPV(w/5% growth)	NPV(w/no growth)	NPV(w/−5% growth)
DCF VALUE	−22,183,132	−22,183,132	−22,183,132
TERMINAL VALUE	−30,127,851	−11,867,208	−7,106,514
NPV	−52,310,983	−34,050,340	−29,289,646

김기영 ───

▌약 력

경기대학교(경영학박사)
전) 영국 Surrey대학 교환교수
한국조리학회 명예회장
한국조리사중앙회 이사
한국외식연감 편찬위원장
혜전대학교 호텔조리과 교수 역임
CIA(미), I.C.I.F(이태리), La Cordon Bieu(프) 다수 국가 조리연수
현) 경기대학교 관광대학 외식조리전공 교수

이재철 ───

▌약 력

경기대학교 관광전문대학원 외식경영학과 석사
경기대학교 일반대학원 외식조리관리학과 박사
전) 호텔롯데 식음팀 근무
세종대학교 사회교육원 와인 마스터 소믈리에과정 수료
가톨릭대학교 커피 바리스타 고급과정 수료
수원여자대학 겸임교수 역임
안산공과대학, 경민대학교, 디지털 서울문화대학, 경기대학교, 건양대학교, 우송대학교
외래교수 역임
현) 혜전대학교 호텔외식조리계열 음료전공 교수

정성훈 ───

▌약 력

성균관대학교 경영학과 졸업, 서강대학교 대학원(경영학 재무관리박사)
전) 증권사 근무
금융연수원, 숭실대, 아주대, 한양대 대학원, 경기대 대학원 등 강사
서강대 경영학과 대우교수, 한국관광공사 전문위원
서울디지털대학교 finance 겸임교수, 아주대학교 경영학과 겸임교수
현) 주택산업연구원 부동산금융 연구위원

▌주요저서 및 역서
『증권투자자들의 투자심리행태』(한국학술정보(주), 2006, 공저)
『인지행위적 재무론』(2006, 공역)
『금융투자와 심리』(2006, 공역)
『투자자가 주의해야 할 20가지 편견』(2007, 공역)
『Valuation of food service related company by using ROV and DCF model』(2008, 공저)
『채권투자분석』(2009, 공저)

- Food & Beverage department -

Valuation of hotel

초판인쇄 | 2009년 4월 15일
초판발행 | 2009년 4월 15일

지은이 | 김기영, 이재철, 정성훈
펴낸이 | 채종준
펴낸곳 | 한국학술정보㈜
주 소 | 경기도 파주시 교하읍 문발리 513-5 파주출판문화정보산업단지
전 화 | 031) 908-3181(대표)
팩 스 | 031) 908-3189
홈페이지 | http://www.kstudy.com
E-mail | 출판사업부 publish@kstudy.com

등 록 | 20,000원
가 격 |

ISBN 978-89-534-1778-6 93320 (Paper Book)
       978-89-534-1779-3 98320 (e-Book)

내일을여는지식 은 시대와 시대의 지식을 이어 갑니다.